PARENTIN

Parenting Teenagers

JOHN AND JANET HOUGHTON

KINGSWAY PUBLICATIONS
EASTBOURNE

Copyright © John and Janet Houghton 1989, 1994
The right of John and Janet Houghton to be identified
as authors of this work has been asserted by them in
accordance with the Copyright, Design
and Patents Act 1988.

First published in 1989 as
So You've Got Teenage Children Too

This revised, enlarged and updated edition 1994

All rights reserved.
No part of this publication may be reproduced or
transmitted in any form or by any means, electronic
or mechanical, including photocopy, recording, or any
information storage and retrieval system, without
permission in writing from the publisher.

Unless otherwise indicated, biblical quotations are from the
New International Version © 1973, 1978, 1984 by the
International Bible Society.

ISBN 0 85476 498 4

Produced by Bookprint Creative Services
P.O. Box 827, BN21 3YJ, England for
KINGSWAY PUBLICATIONS LTD
Lottbridge Drove, Eastbourne, E Sussex BN23 6NT.
Printed in Great Britain

*To all those parents who told us the talks helped
and to Debbie, Sharon and Steve
who bravely endured our efforts at raising them
and who lived to tell the tale.*

Contents

A Letter to All Parents of Teenagers	9
Part One: Conflicts, Chats and Changes	
1. The Ride of Their Lives	13
2. The Dawn of Adolescence	18
3. You Must Change with Them	30
4. Let's Be Friends	40
Part Two: Earrings, Walkmans and Levis	
5. Where Cultures Clash	53
6. Reaction or Revelation?	63
7. Dress to Bless	70
8. The Singer and the Song	75
9. Money, Money, Money	82
10. Discernment	89
Part Three: Love, Sex and Mirages	
11. The Mother of Harlots	97
12. Practise What You Preach	107
13. Keep Sex on the Agenda	114
14. Going Together	126

Part Four: Accidents, Addictions and Academic Agonies
15. Testing Times — 141
16. Hooked! — 156
17. Trouble at School — 168

Part Five: Faith, Fellowship and the Future
18. Passing on the Flame — 179
19. Spiritual Awareness — 194
20. The Will of God — 204

A Letter to All Parents of Teenagers

Dear Long-suffering Parent,

Sometime between eleven and nineteen years ago, in a moment of bright passion, you took part in an amazing piece of genetic engineering. From that secret fusion of sperm and ovum has now emerged this fascinating, devastating, complex being that is your very own teenager.

Have you produced a monster or a marvel? You may well ask. Teenagers often appear to be a curious mixture of our embarrassingly worst and our impressively best traits.

Handling this potent cocktail isn't easy, so you are entitled to a bit of sympathy and a shoulder to cry on. Or perhaps you just need to know that you're not on your own? Would a few tips help as well?

Then welcome to this book.

We invite you to share a few stories and ideas with us over a pint of nerve tonic. So curl up in the snug of your armchair, check that they're not video-recording you, and comfort yourself with the knowledge that there are others out there going through exactly the same things as yourself. More important, with a bit of help it's possible not only to survive teenagers, but you can succeed with them as well.

We've just four qualifications for writing this book.

Three of those are our own children. The other is the decision we took back in 1968.

Having no previous experience, we decided to raise our children by the only text book we believed to be any good—the Bible. The risk was well worth taking. In spite of many trials and tribulations, strong personalities and ideas, God has enabled us to come through happy, secure and fulfilled. Our children grew up to love God and to love us. They truly are among our finest friends.

Teenagers are no problem to God. He loves them and knows exactly how to handle them. He's very willing to help you with yours. Hang on to that nerve tonic and we'll try to show you how!

Sympathetically yours,

John & Janet Houghton

Part One

Conflicts, Chats and Changes

I
The Ride of Their Lives

The sometimes serious, often hilarious and mostly perplexing task of raising teenagers is the most important job any of us will ever do. If we fail here then we really have failed. It's a sober thought in a world troubled by rising juvenile crime, runaway children, acid house raves and death-dealing AIDS.

But be encouraged! There's a welcome paradox to this awesome task. It's this: just when you feel you are failing most, you may in fact be succeeding very well indeed. Here's an example of what we mean. It happened to John.

The June sun was generously bright and warm. We had been about two weeks in our new home. The challenging vista of new people to befriend, fresh opportunities to serve and worthwhile things to do stretched enticingly before us. It felt good to be in the will of God. Then the door crashed open. In stomped one of our daughters.

'Dad, can I speak to you in the garden?' she demanded.

I stiffened. When they need a lot of space, you can bet I need a lot of grace! We went outside. She was bristling like a broom head.

Halfway along the path she unloosed the pent-up torrent.

'Dad, this house is terrible. It's awful! There's something bad about it. Ever since we've moved here nothing has gone right. We all hate it. I'm sure it's the wrong place. And we just wish we had an ordinary dad like other dads. Why are you in the ministry? You've got no time for us. You're always busy. I hate it all. Why have we come here?'

I thought, 'I'm booked to take a conference series on how to raise teenagers in three weeks' time.'

Her voice rose to a nerve-shattering crescendo. 'It's absolutely terrible, Dad,' she screeched. 'I just don't know how we can go on like this. The whole family's falling apart. Don't you understand? Everything's falling apart!'

I looked back at the adjoining houses. They all had their windows open. 'Oh, Lord!' I groaned. 'Shh, don't forget we've got neighbours,' I urged. 'New neighbours!'

'Blow the neighbours,' she screamed. 'That's all you think about. What about me?'

The emotional flood continued for several minutes more.

I gazed at my darling daughter: face red, jaw jutting, fists clenched; taut as a bow. And simmering with frustration. She'd been through a hard time—months of pain, operations, exams and boyfriend troubles had taken their toll. And now the first house move of her life.

You have to look beyond the outside, overcome the hurtful, distorted words, refuse the guilt that breeds despair, reach through the barrier raised by mutually felt pain.

I stretched out my arms to her, spoke some home truths and told her I loved her. She softened, relaxed and put her arms around me. Then she smiled brightly up into my face.

'Thanks, Dad. D'you know, you're the best dad on earth? You've always got time for us when we need you. Thanks ever so much for listening to me. I feel so much better now!'

I gave her a wan smile in return. 'Glad I could help,' I mumbled. 'Um, would you excuse me now? I need to go book my nervous breakdown before the surgery closes for lunch!'

I glanced up at those windows again and hoped the neighbours had heard that last bit she'd said.

That's teenagers for you! One moment it's total disaster and you feel like you've made a terrible mistake somewhere along the line, failed as a parent and lost your child for ever. The next minute, you discover that everything is fine after all. You're the most successful parent who ever lived. And that earth-ripping hurricane was actually just a storm in a teacup viewed through an emotional magnifying glass.

Perhaps we should try to understand what is really going on. It's time for a story. So if you're sitting comfortably....

A bedtime story for parents

Once upon a time, there was a pretty little harbour, and on its sheltered waters bobbed a rubber dinghy containing a contented young child.

On the shore was a lighthouse, and from its window two caring parents kept a watchful eye on their precious offspring.

This happened every day for many happy years, until one fateful day a strange, but not entirely unexpected, current suddenly took hold of the dinghy. All at once, it began to be dragged inexorably towards the harbour entrance. As this was happening, the dinghy began magically to change shape. It grew, and all sorts of bits and pieces began to poke out from all sorts of odd directions. Something was going on!

The dinghy drew closer and closer to the open sea and the current grew stronger and stronger. The mother looked on, horrified. 'My baby!' she cried. 'My baby!' Dad looked very, very worried and said nothing.

The child gripped the sides of his new boat tightly; his face filled with trepidation. He shot a glance back to the security of the lighthouse and wished he was still in his little dinghy.

Then he spied lots of other children out on the high seas, all in boats just like his. They seemed to be managing all right. In fact, many of them were obviously enjoying the choppy waters. 'If they can do it, then so can I,' the child determined.

So, with the harbour walls behind him, the child began the ride of his life. At first he wasn't too sure of the controls, but by copying others, he soon got the hang of them—more or less, anyway. It was great. Far better than that boring old harbour with Mum and Dad always watching.

Not that he forgot his parents, of course. They were still watching, peering anxiously at the high seas. And every so often the child would cast a surreptitious glance in their direction—just to make sure they were still there. In fact, all the children were doing the same with their parents. It's just that nobody wanted to admit it.

It was, however, acceptable to still like your parents. Well, sort of, anyway. So, from time to time, the child would come brumming back into the harbour and demand that his parents come out with him onto the open seas.

Poor parents! Down the steps they'd stagger. Suddenly feeling their age, they'd climb into their own ancient power boat and reluctantly ride out with their child.

However, they got used to it after a fashion and even began to relive something of their own younger days. Riding the waves could still be fun after all.

Then, just as all seemed to be settling down nicely, the child suddenly cried out at them, 'Go away! I don't want you with me any more. I'm not a kid. Why don't you let me live my own life? I want to do things my own way.'

Of course, his parents protested, muttered something inane about relationships and taking an interest, but to little avail. A disdainful snort greeted all their warnings of danger, and before they knew it, their child was off.

This cycle was often repeated and many were the occasions when Mum and Dad returned confused and weary to their lighthouse.

It was after one such episode that disaster struck. The child took on a wave too big for his boat. Just as his parents had predicted, over he went. In spite of their weariness, love and concern ruled the day. They raced to his rescue. Dripping wet, much sobered, they hauled him from the water and took him home.

Now you might have thought he would have learned something from that experience. Apparently not, for the very next day he was out there trying exactly the same manoeuvre all over again. How he managed to stay afloat this time, nobody knows.

This process continued for several heady years, and his parents grew up very quickly! Life was hairy. Then, just as they thought they were about ready to snap, the waters suddenly calmed.

Lo and behold, their child was an adult. They watched with pride as he steered his graceful powerboat in and out of the harbour. He waved to them often now. And sometimes he even taught them a trick or two on the open seas. Life was surprisingly good.

And did they live happily ever after? Well, it depends. But very probably these particular parents did.

There ends our little story. In the following three chapters we'll try to explain what it all means.

2

The Dawn of Adolescence

Chapter 3 of the book known as Ecclesiastes reminds us, 'There is a time for everything, and a season for every activity under heaven.' A time to be born and a time to die; to plant and to uproot; to kill and to heal; to tear down and to build; to weep and to laugh; to mourn and to dance; to scatter and to gather; to embrace and to refrain; to search and to give up; to keep and to throw away; to tear and to mend; to be silent and to speak; to love and to hate; to war and to be at peace.

Note the categories well; the whole lot seems to happen to teenagers all at once! So dramatic are the changes taking place in their lives that it's nothing to find them lurching from love and peace to impending World War Three in no more than a matter of minutes.

A teenager can come off the phone having just mended someone's broken heart and immediately proceed to rip yours to shreds. That irritated refusal to lend a pen to a brother or sister can be instantly followed by a decision to send all their worldly wealth to the relief of Third World poverty. Sullen silence can as easily flip into a non-stop stream of hyperactive one-way conversation embracing world politics, a new hair dye, the ultimate meaning of life and the Maths teacher's latest girlfriend, all in the same breath.

What makes it so frustrating is that these fluctuating moods are largely beyond both their control and ours. The reason for this is simple. They are undergoing some of the most dramatic changes they will ever experience, not only in their bodies but also within their emotions and their environment. And if we protest that we were not as bad as that when we were their age, it is probably because a change is taking place in our own lives, too. It's called middle-aged loss of memory!

Body building, begin!

The vibrant ringing of a biological alarm clock announces the dawn of adolescence. Glands awaken and hordes of hormones pour forth, eager to begin the work of transforming a child into an adult.

Never is a task more zealously, more thoroughly accomplished than by these tireless labourers. Within little more than three or four pubescent years they can stand back to admire their masterpiece. The little girl has become a woman; the boy a man. Together they could found a dynasty.

This activity is usually greeted by a mixture of apprehension and enthusiasm on the part of the human building site that constitutes your child. Girls develop a certain coyness about their bodies, but at the same time they want you to measure their busts. They worry about the irregularity of their periods, but let it be known in a very grown-up manner that it's their 'time of the month'. Boys get embarrassed by their spontaneous erections, but they want you to feel their burgeoning biceps. They peer anxiously at their rudimentary moustaches while celebrating in full, raucous voice the transition from cracked falsetto to basso fortissimo. Both sexes worry unceasingly about their spots.

How well our children manage these changes depends to a large extent on how we have taught them to view their bodies. If the very fact of having a body is considered to be a bit of an embarrassment, something we don't talk about, then your child is likely to have difficulties in coping. Similarly, if the process of change is accompanied by dire warnings about lascivious men and uncontrollable urges, then your child will grow up plagued by unwarranted guilt and fear.

On the other hand, if we as parents respond positively by encouraging and admiring our children's development; if we explain what is happening and assure them that they are normal, then it will be a time of great joy for all concerned. The ability to do this depends on us having a healthy regard for our own bodies.

Sadly, many parents don't. In spite of having lived with their bodies all their lives, they still haven't made friends with them. Maybe they've never liked the shape, or they are ashamed of what they've done with it, or what it does to them. Perhaps they feel it has too many leaks and smells, a bit like an old-fashioned plumbing system. Or possibly they believe that it is, by its very nature, sinful. And all these attitudes they may have picked up from their own parents in the first place.

It helps to remember that Jesus had a body just like ours. His plumbing system was standard issue human grade. He had the same biological needs and urges that we have. And he went through adolescence the same as all teenagers. The only thing he didn't do with his body was use it for sinning.

The fact that the Son of God took real humanity—as the apostle John puts it, 'The Word became flesh'—means that it is neither sinful nor shameful to have a human body.

Furthermore, Christ's death on the cross releases us from the guilt and power of sins committed in the flesh, so that we can use our bodies, including our sexuality, to serve God's will with a clear conscience.

If we have real peace about our own sexuality, we will be well equipped to help our children into a healthy regard for theirs.

We need to make it clear that freedom from shame isn't the same as a lack of modesty. Children have the right to some personal privacy, especially as they develop into adolescence. In our desire to help them accept their bodies, we must not force them into situations where they might feel immodest. For example, they have the right not to be seen naked or partially dressed if they so wish. We should respect that by not barging unwanted into bathrooms or bedrooms. Modesty is still a virtue.

Those hysterical hormones

The suspension system on the average car consists of two components—springs to absorb the bumps, and shock absorbers to damp the recoil of the springs. Without the latter, every bump would cause your car to oscillate wildly; so much so that the occupants would soon become seasick!

The problem our teenagers have is that their emotional shock absorbers are not yet functioning properly. Quite simply, they do not have sufficient experience of life to moderate their feelings. So almost any bump is going to start them oscillating. The bigger the bump, the bigger the bounce. And before long everyone is sick of it—your child included.

'Why do I keep crying?' is a question many parents face from their children around the ages of eleven to thirteen.

Why they also burst out in wild laughter for no apparent reason is one that we ask ourselves.

It has a lot to do with those busy hormones.

Poor men! What they go through once a month, especially if they have daughters as well as a wife. Pre-menstrual tension starts long before a girl has her first period. In fact, you can reasonably date when that will be in the month by plotting those tearful, tense and edgy times. And, whether her periods are regular or erratic, pretty well every month it will be the same, world without end.

Nothing changes. Way back in the book of Genesis, Rachel, hiding some stolen idols by sitting on them, produced the watertight excuse for not being able to arise when her father came looking for them. She just said, in the feminine poetry of the Authorised Version, 'The way of women is upon me.' (Pity about the prosaic NIV rendering, 'I'm having my period.') No man dared argue with her!

In these days when tampon adverts suggest that girls can not only live a normal physical life through their periods, but can do so at an emotional high, we are apt to think that edgy vulnerability is a myth. The truth is, most women appreciate some comfort, support and sympathy at these times.

We're not advocating that girls should take to their beds with the vapours as in a Victorian melodrama. However, to assume that women should charge through life with their bodies and emotions strictly under control is both unreal and a denial of something essentially, preciously feminine. For a girl to feel vulnerable and sensitive is no shame. It is part of what it means to be a woman.

God usually finds it easier to get through to us when we're feeling weak. Not only does he help us in our weaknesses, but he also often has special words for us. It's good then to encourage our girls to pray about their periods and to listen sensitively to the voice of the Lord at those times.

It's tempting, for men especially, simply to retreat to the potting shed until the storm is over. But a loving husband and father will offer understanding and a shoulder to cry on as necessary. It's part of what the apostle Peter meant when he wrote to husbands, 'Be considerate as you live with your wives' (1 Pet 3:7).

Periods are a reality of life for most girls from puberty onwards. Some cope better than others. The reasons for this are complex and have to do with matters ranging over a girl's individual metabolism, her outlook on life, how old she is, current stresses and strains, and the state of her health.

There is some evidence that the addition of B-complex vitamins to the diet can help. Going on the Pill is also a useful way of stabilising periods. This latter decision obviously has to take other matters into consideration.

It will greatly help if you can teach your daughter not to accept the popular view that periods are the curse. It just isn't true. Periods are a God-ordained cleansing of the body in preparation for childbirth. Hence, though inconvenient, they should be looked upon as a reminder of the greatest gift he has given to us: the ability to reproduce ourselves.

Hormonal changes, also to some degree cyclical, affect boys somewhat differently. True, on occasions they cry inexplicably as well, but they're more likely to become morose during these times. Beware—they can rip the doors off their hinges! You say, 'Be careful,' but they don't know what you're talking about. Sullen strength, inner seething without knowing why, is difficult to live with—not to say hazardous.

You never quite know when this emotional terrorism is

going to erupt. Without warning the door will crash open, the house will shudder and the family cat will bolt for safety beneath the sideboard. In stalks your son, face glowering, eyes ranging for a suitable target. It's you or the sofa. If you're sitting on the sofa at the time, it's both.

The bomb explodes. Out pours an irrational flood of highly charged words, the force of which leaves you temporarily speechless. Your innocent sofa gasps under the pummelling of your son's fists. Then, just as suddenly, it's over. He retreats to the hills leaving you shell-shocked and, like your poor old sofa, wondering what on earth you had done to deserve all this.

It's male hormones. Attack and withdraw. The shock absorbers aren't yet functioning properly. Pray for the day when things settle down, and don't buy a new sofa until they do!

Boys and girls are affected by their hormonal changes. Both will have their histrionics at times; both will also on occasions withdraw completely.

'Why are you always sitting in your room? Have we got leprosy?' you protest. They can't tell you. Why did you sit in your room when you were their age? Sometimes our children withdraw for no other reason than that they feel temporarily blue because of their seesawing hormones. At such times, coping with normal, balanced, reasonable people like us is the last thing they can stand!

To be or not to be?

Our modern teenagers are the most media-manipulated, socially-stereotyped and peer-pressured individuals in all history. As a result, they are faced with having to make a phenomenal number of decisions, many of which will affect not only what they'll do, but also who they will become.

'Hey, teenager. What's your lifestyle going to be? Are you going to study, or not? Chosen your exam options yet? You going to work or go on the dole? When are you going to get a girlfriend? Condoms or the Pill? Where do you buy your gear? What do you think of Sexbusters' new single? You ain't gonna vote, are you? Why don't you leave home? Religious? You're kidding! How do you know you're not gay? Bought any shares yet?'

One of the very salient points made by the social commentator, Alvin Toffler, is that overchoice can lead to panic, mental breakdown and ultimately to chronic apathy.

We needed to buy a new jug-kettle recently—a fairly simple task, we thought. But there are dozens of the wretched things. They all look more or less the same, yet you know they can't be, otherwise there wouldn't be so many different models, would there?

So which is the best?

They have high wattage and low wattage, balls that go up and down, two balls that go up and down, colour co-ordinated or plain white—with a pastel hint, designer-shaped or functional lines, big ones, small ones, fuel-miser ones, lights that go on when it's boiling, lights that go off when it's boiling, switches that glow in the dark, plugs that self-eject in emergency; kettles that cure all known diseases, that self-destruct in the event of alien attack or when peed on by the cat, that resolve your love life and do all the housework for you. If only we could find one that would boil water!

After a bemused hour spent gazing at all these options we just clung to one another, exhausted, gibbering, vacant-eyed wrecks of what were once noble human beings. We would have welcomed with open arms the men in white coats at that point—or at least a nice cup of tea.

Our children can suffer similar effects when they confront the barrage of lifestyle options offered to them. With little experience of life, in a culture that despises traditional wisdom and which is in any case changing rapidly, they must decide their own futures. Not surprisingly, many teenagers show symptoms of premature stress as they fret over their choices. Others simply cannot make up their own minds, so are for ever chopping and changing their opinions. Sadly, many more lapse into apathy. They merely conform to mediocrity, taking the path of least resistance—and least hope.

We've noticed that although most parents anticipate difficulties arising from change in the early teenage years, fewer seem prepared for another crisis point around the ages of sixteen to seventeen. Yet this is a particularly difficult time for many children. The problem once more is overchoice. It's the time when they're perhaps leaving school, wondering about work, maybe under examination pressure. Do they go to college, university, technical college, or stay on at school? Do they get married? Who do they vote for? Do they go into debt by taking on loans? Should they learn to drive? Be prepared for some interesting discussions.

Some children manage choices very well. That may be because they are born with naturally decisive temperaments. It is more likely to be because of how three other factors operate in their lives.

Peer group pressure

Peer pressure is a term often used in a negative manner, but a supportive peer group can be a tremendous asset for a child. All the talk such a group indulges in about the opposite sex, about jobs and cars, fashions and travel, that we might think is idle chatter is really a process of discovery. It is a chance to consider options in the company of friends. Lack of this is the reason lone children find good decision-making that much harder.

Choosing friends isn't easy; choosing good friends is even harder. It's something that requires much prayer on our part. We can't force friendship. What we can do is to encourage our children in the right direction.

One of the values of good youth organisations and church youth clubs is that they provide just this sense of teamwork in the game of life. Importantly, a well-run group provides a good moral and spiritual framework where our children can explore their options without the danger of being enticed down destructive paths.

Self-worth

'Identity crisis' is a piece of modern jargon, used to cover everything from 'Who am I?' to 'Where shall we go for our holidays?' What matters for our children is that they should feel good when they think about themselves. Such self-acceptance comes from within; from knowing that you are loved by God and by others. It arises from an acceptance of one's limitations and an appreciation of one's assets.

How important it is to encourage our children throughout their lives. Jan recalls the occasion when she collected one of our children from playschool just prior to Mother's Day. The children had all painted pictures with the caption, 'I love you, Mummy.' One little girl ran to her mother waving her picture with that innocent desire to please. To Jan's horror, the girl's mother screwed up the picture and dismissed her brusquely with the words, 'I haven't time for all that rubbish!'

It doesn't take too many cruel actions of that kind to give a child a major problem.

If our children have been steadily and realistically encouraged by us throughout their lives, they are unlikely to undergo anything that can really be called an identity crisis. They will, consequently, be well placed for making decisions.

Wise counsel

Our society is strong on knowledge, but very short of wisdom, by which we mean acquiring skills for life. What little is on offer is so often based upon relative values rather than truth. As a consequence, the reference points on the map of life appear to be more like drifting balloons in an ocean of drowning people than signposts for the wise wayfarer.

So where is wise, reliable counsel to come from? Primarily, from us their parents. The teenager who can communicate easily with loving parents has a tremendous advantage over one who can't. We can't stress enough the importance of being available to our children for when they need us. That means being around and talking to them even when they apparently don't need us at any profound level. Walks, sport, cooking together, shopping, all provide times when we are at least there to offer advice if they want it.

Again, a good church has much to offer. Teenagers should feel that they have free access to pastors and youth leaders, as well as other older Christians. We parents mustn't feel our noses are being put out of joint over this. Often a child needs to speak with someone who is less emotionally involved than we are, simply to gain a wider perspective on a problem.

We must not blame our children for what isn't their fault. They are changing and they can't help it. The pressures, physically, emotionally and socially are considerable. They need our support and understanding, not simply our reaction to their reactions.

We should encourage our children that God is in control of their lives. Psalm 31:15 says, 'My times are in your hands; deliver me from my enemies and from those who pursue me.'

Teach them that their teenage years, tumultuous though they seem, are in God's hands. When they're trying to make decisions about their careers, when there is too much homework, when they are in such a social whirl that they can't keep up with it, their times are in God's hands. And so, mercifully, are ours.

3
You Must Change with Them

This may come as a bit of a shock. You've got your husband-and-wife act together, the rent/mortgage is almost bearable, you feel settled in your job and are just beginning to enjoy some of those little comforts in life that make it all seem worthwhile. You may even feel relieved that your children are now old enough not to need you every five minutes of the day. Ah, bliss! You can relax, indulge in what you most want to do, and settle down into your cosy, Dralon-lined rut.

Not a bit of it. We have to change along with our teenagers. Otherwise we will lose them, and live to regret it.

Change is always uncomfortable, especially when we are just beginning to hope for domestic peace. It's made more so by the fact that we're not so young as we were. We're usually at least in our thirties by the time our kids hit their teens. We may be in our forties or even fifties.

On top of that, the domestic bliss we desire is often counterbalanced by this being a time of life when fathers are working hard for the promotion that will make their middle years secure. For many Christians it is also a period when church may involve considerable lay leadership responsibilities.

Then you look at your kids and their culture. You freeze

with horror. Whatever happened to the Beatles, Elvis and The Who? The generation gap, as we used to call it, now begins to look like the Grand Canyon. We're not as 'with it' as we used to be and we're not sure we have the energy to start trying to understand an alien youth culture, where promiscuity isn't even a dare tinged with guilt, but a matter-of-fact way of saying goodnight.

How then must our role change? What must happen to those former guardians of the harbour?

A lighthouse

We must become a lighthouse to our teenagers. Jesus said:

> You are the light of the world. A city on a hill cannot be hidden. Neither do people light a lamp and put it under a bowl. Instead they put it on its stand, and it gives light to everyone in the house. In the same way, let your light shine before men, that they may see your good deeds and praise your Father in heaven (Mt 5:14–16).

It is so important that we 'shine' in front of our teenagers because at no other time in life are they looking so perceptively at our lifestyle as now. Even when we're not aware of it, perhaps especially then, they are observing with a critical eye the way we live. Their sensors are searching for even the slightest whiff of hypocrisy.

Sometimes they will be quite openly critical of us, pointing out our faults, challenging our dearest-held values, ridiculing our ideas. They will ask difficult questions about our faith, and we may be tempted to think they're going to reject Christianity wholesale.

It's very tempting to react. We can start criticising them in return, and knock their newly emerging values. 'Call that music? You're not going out looking like that, are you?

How can you be so naïve? Any fool with an ounce of common sense knows better than that. And your room's like a pig-sty!' And so on. It's a sure recipe for disaster and a flagrant invitation to open rebellion.

The questionings our children have, even the criticisms, do not mean that they are automatically rejecting everything we have ever taught them. Indeed, the opposite. It's a sign that they are taking the challenge of our lifestyle seriously. What they're doing is testing to see whether our values are any good. Can they stand up to real questions? Are they sufficient for another, different generation?

Here's a typical example. Young Gilly comes home to her happily married mum. 'What's the point of marriage?' she exclaims. 'All everyone does is get divorced. Why go through with it? It's more honest just to live together.'

Immediately, Mum panics. 'What about all we've taught her?' she wails. 'Is our daughter going to start sleeping around? Perhaps she is already and this is her way of letting us know.'

However, ask where the idea came from. The answer is usually obvious. Either a school teacher who doesn't know any better than to teach that weary old ethic from the sixties, or schoolmates whose own parents have broken up, or some commercial teenage magazine/radio station that rattles on glibly about 'honesty' in relationships.

We've heard it all before—it's what we were taught. Only in our youth the ideas were still fresh; now they're just foolish.

But don't go on about it like that just now. A 'sane lecture' will evoke some response like, 'You just don't understand,' and Gilly will probably storm off to her room.

Better to say, 'Yes, dear,' and, 'Well, I still love Daddy

very much,' and leave it at that. There *are* times for serious discussion, of course. But this isn't one of them.

From this time on, if not before, Gilly is watching her parents' marriage. She will compare it with the marriages, or lack thereof, of her friends' parents. The answers to her questions are demonstrated before her eyes—you don't have to be *un*married to be in love.

Some of the questions they ask can be very difficult to answer. It's made worse by the fact that they may not have sufficient experience even to appreciate the answer. What are we to do? Ask for divine wisdom, of course. We mustn't just quote scriptures or clichés—that goes almost without saying. Much of the time it's not so much the answer they're interested in as the manner in which we respond. They know better than we what is happening when we react intensely by raising our voices or laying down the law. It's like the prompt found in the margin of the preacher's notes—'Shout loud, argument weak!'

Better be a lighthouse than a foghorn.

A powerboat

Our children need our companionship. There are times when they really want us to ride the waves with them.

Sometimes they want us to go shopping with them. It can be a terrifying experience. You head instinctively in the direction of C&A's or Marks & Spencer's. They hate both. So you are dragged, protesting feebly, into Bums 'n' Boobs Lovemachine, an overpriced emporium characterised by pounding rock, wild flashing strobes and freakish sales assistants dropping fag ash over the racks of garish tat that passes for modern fashion. You suddenly feel about ninety years old and, worse still, have that terrible feeling they're all looking at you and wondering what Gran or Gramps is doing here in the first place.

Your kids love it. They try on this and that, want to know what you think, totally ignore your inane mumblings, want *you* to try it on and laugh loudly at the result. And at the end of the day you come out, having spent all the Family Allowance for the week on one tatty bit of rag that they're going to wear for about two days before they hate it—just like you said in the first place.

What have you done to deserve all this, you ask as you reach for another handful of tranquillisers? Ah, but you're riding with them and that's the important thing. Companionship is worth the cost.

Discussing careers is another powerboat area.

When John was at school he had to fill in a careers form. So he put down nuclear physicist or mountain guide. He didn't want to be either really—just trying it on—though he says he finished up as a mountain guide.

Our kids come up with the most incredible ideas, don't they? Hardly surprising when they're given so many options to choose from these days. Couple that with the pressure to obtain qualifications, and it's not surprising that our discussions with them are likely to take us into much that is frankly unrealistic territory. But they need us to join in the explorations none the less.

'If I give up Maths and French—the teachers are no good anyway—and take up Art, I could start painting pictures and sell them. Then I could use the money to go to Central America and write an illustrated book about Mayan civilisation. I've been interested in that ever since I saw that programme on the telly last week. And I'm OK at English 'cos I got a B in the last test. I expect you'd have to help me out with the plane fare, though. But I'll pay you back when the book's published!'

Let them explore. Don't just say that it's a lot of rubbish. Encourage your children not to fall into the ruts set by society. Let them be adventurous in their ideas.

However, we also have to challenge them. 'Um, sounds interesting. Tell you what, why not paint one or two pictures in your spare time and see how much money you get for them? And get a book from the library on the Mayans to see what the competition is like.'

Or, to the would-be brain surgeon, 'Are you being realistic about this? Do you really want to spend seven years qualifying to be a doctor when you got minus fifteen in your last Maths exam and they kicked you out of the Biology class for "liberating" all the white rats? And we're still paying for that explosion in the Chemistry lab. Are you sure this is your calling?'

Ultimately the unpalatable truth is that qualifying for most jobs requires some sort of perseverance, be that in making applications, going for interviews, or obtaining academic qualifications. We have to ride with our kids, challenging, encouraging, until they can see for themselves what they really want to do—and what in reality they could do.

It is fascinating to see how Jesus 'powerboated' with his disciples when he fed the five thousand. Matthew 14 records the story.

A great crowd had followed Jesus and spent the day listening to him. He appeared to be oblivious to their physical needs and come evening his responsible disciples in a show of maturity, just like our teenagers when they're hungry, suggested that as it was getting late he should dismiss the crowd so they could all get something to eat.

Jesus responded by giving them the opportunity to take the initiative. 'They do not need to go away. You give them something to eat.' Take the lead. Think out how you're going to do it.

That set them muttering among themselves. 'What have we got? Five measly loaves and two glorified fish fingers. You're joking. What's he expect us to do with that? How can we feed this lot with five loaves and two fish?' That's the point at which they faced reality.

Then Jesus stepped in. 'Bring them here to me. Direct the people to sit down on the grass.' Ah, they can manage that.

He takes the bread and the fish, gives thanks and breaks the loaves. He's full of faith. One day they will be, but not yet.

It would have been tempting at this point for Jesus, having shown up the immaturity of his disciples, to have carried on without their assistance. Imagine how they would have felt left standing idly by, trying to look cool to disguise their sense of inadequacy, while he got on with the job. Jesus was a better 'parent' than that. He involved them again. 'You go and give it to the people,' he said.

Yet Jesus didn't simply create a mountain of bread and fish for them to distribute. The disciples were intimately involved in the miraculous process. Somewhere between his hands giving to them, and they to the crowds, the food multiplied. Instead of feeling foolish, they were privileged to take part in an amazing example of divine power.

When to challenge, when to help, when to entrust. That's powerboating wisdom.

If we would follow Jesus' example, then we will have to take some risks with our kids. Now it sounds very mature to say that we should give our children freedom commensurate with their sense of responsibility, but that idea is, in fact, unworkable. It leaves us in a dilemma:

they're not very responsible, so I can't give them any more freedom; but if I don't give them more freedom, how will they learn to be responsible?

What we actually have to do is to increase their freedom beyond their responsibility, but in measured doses. In other words, we must allow them to make mistakes. Our job is to ensure that they don't have so much liberty that the mistake turns into an absolute disaster. The pattern is: risk → mistake or success → increased responsibility → risk again—and so on.

The best example we can think of is learning to drive a car. It's no use waiting until the pupil is responsible before you risk venturing on to the road, otherwise you'd spend the rest of your days parked in the driveway. Instead, the instructor/pupil relationship is one of controlled risk, with a view to progressively reducing the control until the pupil has full responsibility for the vehicle.

That's how people mature. Jesus understood it. 'One day,' he said to his disciples, 'you will do greater works than I do.'

A lifeboat

There are times when we have to transform ourselves into lifeboats.

Mike and Jean's teenage son decided to run away from home. They were good parents, nothing awful had happened at home, but their son was going through a complicated time of life. He suddenly felt he wanted to be free, to escape.

The police found him eventually and phoned his parents. They drove down to fetch him. The same story repeats itself a thousand times over. How are they to respond to him when they meet up?

It's tempting to be angry, or to lecture, or even to counsel. You enter the police station and say, 'Thank God we found you. We're so glad you're all right.' Then you get him in the car and it starts, 'You know your mum and I were very upset by you running off. It's been a nasty shock and your mum has had to go to the doctor because of her nerves. She's been given tranquillisers. And I've had to take time off work. And that's not easy for me at this time of year. For all that, we do forgive you, but we think you ought to learn some lessons out of this. And we want to try to get to the bottom of why you did it.'

This is the wrong approach altogether. Your runaway kid is full to the throat with conflicting emotions. He's relieved, but sorry. He feels guilty, but a bit resentful. He's glad you came, but may well feel that you're the reason he went in the first place. And nothing has changed. He needs time and space to think, and a chance to say what he really feels.

It's better to do what the father did in the story of the prodigal son. Welcome your child back. Have a celebration because he's come home. Time for deep chats later—when he's ready for it.

Fortunately, most of our rescue operations will be less dramatic than this. The issues are far more likely to be matters such as getting refunds from shops, or asking a Year Head to change a wrongly chosen study option. Or, of course, it may be because a friendship has broken down. On this, you may think they should never have entered the relationship to start with. But that's not the point now. Your child is hurt, depressed and feeling lonely. Mum and Dad to the rescue!

When to be a lighthouse, or a powerboat, or a lifeboat

needs wisdom. In other words, as the saying goes, it requires a flexible response to the situation. This is no time for us to get set in our ways. We have to fight the moral flab of middle years and keep at the spiritual aerobics. And you never know, we may even grow to like it.

4
Let's Be Friends

There are times when beacon-flashes of light illuminate our path for a brief instant, and in those moments we see the otherwise hidden signpost that shows us the direction we should take. It's called revelation. Such was our experience when Debbie, our eldest, was approaching her teens. And on our signpost were written the words, 'Become friends.'

At first we didn't altogether understand it. After all, we already loved our daughter and had a very happy relationship with her. Then we remembered the words of Jesus to his disciples, 'I no longer call you servants.... Instead, I have called you friends' (Jn 15:15). The change marked not only the growing confidence Jesus had in his disciples' grasp of truth, but also his desire for an adult relationship with them. And, as the Master, it was his prerogative to initiate this.

We understood then that we must initiate a similar change in our relationship with our children. The mum and dad of childhood must become the friends of the emerging adult. But what did that involve?

Consult and confide

The first thing we discovered was that we had to command less and to consult more. When children are young, we tell them what to do and we expect them quite properly to obey us. If they refuse, we have various ways of enforcing our will over theirs. Successful parents ensure that Mum and Dad win on all the important matters. That's fine for children.

However, it's not the way to treat friends. Start commanding your friends, with threats of sanctions if they don't obey, and they won't be your friends for long. Friendship is based upon goodwill, upon a freely agreed consensus of ideas. Friends discuss and come to a mutual understanding, because that is what both parties want. They do what they agree is the best thing all round.

That is what it means to become friends with our children. We begin to treat them as adults and to take them into our confidence. When they ask, 'Why?', instead of replying, 'Because I say so,' we reason with them. (You may always have done this with your children. The difference now is that you expect them to understand your reasons.) We explain our position. We ask what they think and take that into account in our decision making.

Another thing we do with our friends is to share our feelings with them. When children are young, it's inappropriate to unburden our hearts onto them. But as they move towards adulthood, it's a good and necessary thing to do.

We are not suggesting by this that they should be overloaded. After all, they still have a very limited experience of life. Certainly it is unwise to share marriage problems with young teens, for example. Such matters require adult counsel. And if you're a single parent, then be careful not to lay too many of the problems of loneliness onto your child because that may only increase the child's own sense of isolation. You need to talk to brothers and sisters in the church about those problems.

Having said that, most children respond very well when we drop the parental masks and let them know how we really feel. It helps if you can say, 'Sorry, I'm feeling under the weather today,' or, 'We've just had a big bill and we're not sure at the moment if we can afford to pay it,' or, 'Actually, I'm feeling very hurt over what Auntie May said on the phone yesterday.'

Our own children pray for us because they are aware of our feelings and we've made known to them what our needs are. In fact, we ask them to pray for us. And very often they gain a spiritual insight denied to us. Revelation does not come according to age.

Of course, this easy-going mutual friendship doesn't happen overnight. There are still times in early teens when Mum and Dad have to lay down the law. And children aren't always receptive to being treated as adult confidantes. It will take several years before, all being well, you have a full adult relationship with them. And you may not evolve out of having to dictate bedtimes and the acceptable state of their rooms until they are all of eighteen. The important thing is to observe the signpost and make the initial commitment to change.

Time and space

Let's be honest about it. If friendship is to happen we must give our teenagers time. Sitting watching TV with them (the staple opiate of the masses) doesn't count, unless perhaps you use the time to discuss the values being communicated, or the programme serves as a means of giving the family a real laugh together.

We mean time when you can talk, when you can share, when you can grow to understand and appreciate one another.

It would be no exaggeration to say that we have felt on occasions that our children's whole future turned upon us being there at the right time. That only really happens if we are already committed to making them a genuine priority in our lives.

Unless we spend time 'by the wayside'—playing sport, walking together, cooking together, visiting places—true friendship will never develop. It's no use sitting a child in an armchair and saying, 'We need to talk! Let's now talk!' Such an artificial approach to conversation is doomed from the start.

Real communication takes place not when we are 'working at our relationship', but as a by-product of some shared activity. The rise of so much counselling these days is a reflection on the loss of easy-going friendship where people shared their hearts and received advice without scarcely being aware that it was happening.

This kind of time is the most precious gift we can bestow on our children.

Letting off steam

Spending time with our children in a developing adult friendship will not necessarily be the easiest of matters. We knew a man once who complained that his biggest problem in this area was simply coping with the immature ideas and feelings of his young teenage daughter. How do you develop an intelligent relationship with a child who comes out with sentences like, 'I've decided I want to be a social worker and I want to live in a forest miles from anyone, 'cos I'm fed up with people!'

The secret is not to take such statements too seriously. If we wade in as parents with, 'Stop talking such nonsense, you silly child!' we'll soon put paid to friendship. Extreme ideas in teenagers simply reflect a lack of experience. Immaturity, as we keep emphasising, is not sin and therefore shouldn't be rebuked as though it was.

We might do well also to remember that the truth often lies at the extremes. The danger of being mature and 'balanced' is that, as with the midpoint of a seesaw, there's no movement at all. Our safe world may, in fact, be static and thus actually false to the truth about life. Teenagers often see that better than we do. Hence, their willingness to experiment with ideas, be they ever so wild.

All children need the opportunity to let off steam, especially teenagers. Sooner or later they'll do it anyway, but when you sense a head of steam building up, you might try this for an idea. Go for a walk with your child, or sit with him in his room, wherever he's relaxed, and say something like this: 'Listen, Mike, I want you to feel free to say anything you like about anything you want. Blow your top! If you're fed up with me, if you're fed up with your mum, if you're fed up with your brothers and sisters, fed up with school or church, if you hate the pastor, then you can say so. Even if you feel like hating God, say so. I'm not going to condemn you, punish you, or correct you. Let rip and say what you like!'

You will probably never have rebellious teenagers if you provide them with such opportunities from time to time. Rebellion is born out of inner frustration. It comes from the feeling that one has no choice, no say in what is happening, or even the right to complain.

Just recently we came across a sixteen-year-old boy who kept walking out of church in the middle of the meeting. It wasn't that he didn't wish to be there; simply that his parents gave him no choice. They failed to hear his feelings about the subject. If only they would say one Sunday morning, 'Why don't you stay in bed and give church a miss today?' He might actually do that for one Sunday, but he would probably be back the next, by his own free choice. Instead, every Sunday, he'd come along with all those bottled-up feelings and express them in the only way he knew how.

The Bible says, 'In your anger do not sin' (Eph 4:26). To let our children clear everything out of their system on occasions is not to make them sin. And in any case, if they do go a bit over the top, they'll be more aware of it than you. Leave them to sort it out with God. He has a good reputation for understanding. After all, he's coped with psalmists who came up with such edifying gems as, 'Break the teeth in their mouths, O God,' and, 'Happy shall he be who takes your little ones and dashes them against the rock!' Nothing if not an honest expression of how they felt!

Your children may want to be angry about hush-hush subjects in your church, such as, 'If God's a God of love, why is there all this suffering in the world? Why isn't our church doing anything about Somalia? Why aren't the older folk as thrilled with Jesus as we are? Why are there people in our church who read the *Daily Express*? Why aren't we praying for Northern Ireland in our meetings? Why are all the deacons so old? And why is Mr Jones allowed to be one when he's so miserable?'

There have been many occasions when we have been quite sobered by allowing our children to be really honest with us; times when we have needed to repent; times when we have realised that we were blind. We parents need the humility to learn. It is tempting for us to think our children are being unfair, unbalanced and unloving when they pour out their feelings. But just listen, and later meditate on what they have said. They might have a point. And we may need to say sorry.

When it hurts

Friendship inevitably involves some hurts born out of misunderstanding, thoughtlessness and disagreement. In fact, the closer you get to somebody, the higher the risk of this happening. This is why marriage is the most blessed of human relationships, but at the same time also the hardest to succeed at. The mark of a healthy relationship is not that you never have problems, but that you know how to resolve them.

We've already noted Ephesians 4:26. It says, 'In your anger do not sin. Do not let the sun go down while you are still angry, and do not give the devil a foothold.'

Not letting the sun go down on our wrath is the secret. For husbands and wives it means never going to sleep with back-to-back fellowship. Never, ever. We think we can say with integrity that in twenty-eight years of marriage we have never succeeded in going to sleep with an unresolved issue. Not that we haven't tried on occasions, of course! It means we have been preserved from resentment and bitterness in our relationship.

We must do the same with our teenagers. It's a bit harder with them because we no longer put them to bed, nor do we share the same room. It's much easier to have a row and simmer in front of the TV while they go to their room, not to be seen until the next morning. We parents have to take the initiative in reconciliation. That's the responsibility of the stronger party.

It involves being the first to say sorry. The issue may not have been your fault, but the fact that it developed into a row is both your faults, so start the apologising. The word 'sorry' probably contains more power to win teenagers than any other in the English language. Ultimately it doesn't really matter whose fault it was. After all, you're not Trade Unionists trying to negotiate percentages at the bargaining table. The important issue is that you and your child are out of fellowship. The goal is reconciliation before sundown. It's no use waiting until they come and say sorry. Why should they? They feel as hurt as you do. And you're the mature one! So you initiate it. That's the way to win your children's hearts.

Breaking the curse

We don't believe it is necessary for Christian children to be either wimps or rebels. It's perfectly possible to raise children with robust characters who will stick right with you throughout their teenage years. In fact, that is one of the promises of the gospel.

The last words of the last book in the Old Testament anticipate a day coming when parents and children will be reconciled. 'See, I will send you the prophet Elijah before that great and dreadful day of the Lord comes. He will turn the hearts of the fathers to their children, and the hearts of the children to their fathers; or else I will come and strike the land with a curse' (Mal 4:5–6).

Good relationships between parents and their teenagers are a prophetic mark of the New Covenant and a sign that the kingdom of God has come. In a nation which is so clearly under a curse for lack of this, there can scarcely be a more important issue.

When most of us were teenagers there were the beginnings of what was called the 'generation gap'. A wedge was being driven between parents and children. Different values, different cultures and the breakdown of relationships. Home life began to disintegrate. Today it has reached crisis level with a vast number of broken homes and countless shattered relationships between parents and their children that constitute the major social problem of our time. A curse has smitten the land, and we must heal it.

That healing begins in our own homes. There is no point in preaching the gospel on street corners, attending prayer meetings and conferences, singing great songs and knowing all there is to know about the faith, if we're not friends with our kids. This has to be the priority of our lives.

Some of us may feel we struggle with it, perhaps almost to the point of despair. Renew your faith! Pray that God will annul the curse in your family. Recognise what is going on in your children's lives. Be understanding. Get close to them, however inconvenient it seems at times. Show them that they are loved and accepted. Let them know that you want their friendship. And God will honour you.

Others of us are cut to the quick by all this. We know that we are seriously out of relationship with our children. The Holy Spirit is convicting us urgently that we should take the initiative in putting matters right. It's not easy, but it is essential that we reach out before it becomes too late. The barriers harden. Love can be lost for ever. Reaching out through our own pride and pain costs, but the price is worth it if it means reconciliation, forgiveness and healing all round.

Homework

Here is some simple homework. Just ask each of your teenagers these three questions, and take note of the answers. We suggest that each parent does this separately and then compares notes.

Question 1: What makes you happiest about me?
Question 2: What irritates you most about me?

Question 3: What would you most like to see improved or changed in our relationship?

It's important that you listen when you do this. Ask your child what he or she means by their answer if it isn't clear, but don't disagree with them. This is their opportunity to say what they feel. You must not be defensive, otherwise they will either clam up, or this constructive exercise will turn into a row.

Be grateful to God for what they like about you. Be sobered by what they don't like. And ask for their ideas about how you might together initiate some improvements in the relationship. You may be surprised at how good their suggestions are.

Part Two

Earrings, Walkmans and Levis

5
Where Cultures Clash

Someone once said that the secret of managing a hot potato is to keep it in the air most of the time. That is perhaps how you'll feel about our approach to this next section, as we juggle with the conflict that arises between secular culture and our Christian counter-culture. For there are no easy answers to the problem of being 'in the world but not of the world', and even less so when it comes to guiding our children through the maze of cultural options confronting them today.

For many parents it is a potato that becomes too hot to handle, and differences of opinion over such matters as music, clothes, reading material, television, video games, alcohol and smoking become major sources of argument with their teenagers—so much so that these issues may undermine the whole relationship.

The reason for this is simple: culture is very personal. It affects our tastes, our values and beliefs, and our hopes and fears. So we feel strongly about the issue—especially when someone else's culture intrudes into our space, for example when Madonna is blaring from your child's bedroom and your preference is for Dire Straits, the Beatles, or even Beethoven.

Added to which, the conflict between Christianity and secularism is a real one. This issue is more than one of taste—it is also to do with truth. The apostle John says, 'We know that we are children of God, and that the whole world is under the control of the evil one' (1 Jn 5:19). It's hardly surprising then that we should want to protect our children from 'the world'.

However, we cannot withdraw from it. For one thing, God calls us to be salt and light, and that means dwelling confidently in the midst of society, just as Jesus did. Furthermore, we cannot say that it is all bad. That would be to deny God's creation and his undoubted blessings upon even unbelieving mankind. Do you refuse to eat ice cream because it was invented by non-Christians? Or do you not shop in an arcade designed by pagan architects? We have to live in the real world as best we can. That means holding to what is good, refusing what is evil, and changing things for the better wherever we have the opportunity.

It's a complex task and it's little wonder we sometimes get our fingers burned when we try to get a grip on this particular potato.

Christians used to talk about worldliness, by which they meant the bad side of secular culture—though for some it meant everything that wasn't church culture. But, if we still use such a term, what do we mean by it? Is Brahms any less worldly than Pink Floyd? Are discos more worldly than jazz or folk clubs, or pubs more worldly than restaurants? Is 'toplessness' abroad more worldly than wearing a bikini at home? Does Jackie Collins really write in a more worldly fashion than Agatha Christie did?

Many parents would like simple yes/no answers to such matters. A published list of decrees from headquarters would solve the problem. Just look it up in the book. Prescribed music, fashions and reading matter for the year would surely make life easier.

Or would it? Life frankly isn't that simple. The plain fact

is that the legalistic approach doesn't work—not least because there are so many things the Bible doesn't pronounce upon. It's not possible, for example, to decree the biblical length of a skirt or whether studded leather jackets are in order. The moment we start attempting to produce our authorised lists on such matters, we move away from revelation and on to personal opinion. Not surprisingly, our kids may feel every right to challenge our authority on the subject.

Instead, we must seek to understand and to apply the principles of God's word to our contemporary world. By thus becoming wise and discerning ourselves, we'll be able to show our children the timeless relevance of the Scriptures to the issues of their own lives and so teach them to live pure, free and fulfilled in Christ. We'll also greatly reduce the occasions for conflict between us and them. And that can't be bad.

However, before we explore this path, we should take note of the secular cultural terrain through which we are presently passing. It is surprisingly religious.

The cult of 'outerness'

Most of the culture that influences our teenagers comes from one common source—be it New York or New Orleans, London or Liverpool, modern culture originates in the city. Nowadays, provincial towns and country villages, once strong sources of culture and community themselves, bow to the all-prevailing influence of the city's style.

It is, in fact, a relatively small caucus of city-focused media people that influences the lives of millions of today's young people. Deeply committed to the same beliefs, promoting their own image and type, their ideas pour out endlessly through the television, the radio, newspapers and magazines. So successful has this been that, in spite of the vast differences in children's personalities, there is today a veneer of cultural 'teenagerness' which is recognisably the same in almost any part of the nation.

It has produced what we choose to call the cult of 'outerness'—the adoption of images, fashions, lifestyles and values, not because these have been thought through by our kids, or even been handed down from previous generations, but simply because this is what the media hype decrees is 'in'.

Here is a trivial but typical example of what we mean in the realm of fashion. A few years ago Levis brought out jeans that have buttons instead of a zip. Why? During our far-off childhood, the zip superseded buttons because zips are more reliable and look better. (They may present a threat to certain parts of the male anatomy, but are considerably less embarrassing than the dreaded missing button.) Why return to a redundant technology? Because somebody came up with the novel idea of doing so. A gimmick, no less, which the manufacturers hoped would sell more of their product.

And no doubt it did, because the new-style jeans were raunchily promoted as what every cool customer should be wearing. Subliminal images of youthfulness, ego-enhancement and increased sexual attractiveness—underlying which is a value system quite unperceived by the average buyer—all served to convince him that he must have this product.

The Levis advertising machine is only one aspect of the whole. People are constantly being persuaded to adopt the latest music or make-up, paperback morality or consumer novelty, without ever really understanding what is going on. Never before has a generation been so manipulated and conditioned by the mass media as today. Young people, your world is ruled, and you know not by whom, or how, or why.

At first sight this might seem harmless enough. After all, vulnerable as they are, most children don't grow up that bad. And it surely isn't wrong to wear Levis. But all the time there is a subtle conditioning taking place—a gentle, pleasurable urging to conform to the status quo of the image-makers. And beneath that lies something more sinister.

Imagine, if you will, the gods of this age. They are invisible. They have no shape or form. But they have their teachers, their evangelists and a multitude of worshippers enticed into service at an ever-earlier age. They take the place of Christ.

We'll have a brief look at three of them.

Romanticism—the goddess of sex and violence

In 2 Samuel 13 we have recorded one of the most sordid stories in the Bible. It is the tale of Amnon and Tamar. The first verse sets the scene. 'In the course of time, Amnon son of David fell in love with Tamar, the beautiful sister of Absalom son of David.' Tamar was Amnon's half-sister. His love for her was incestuous.

Incestuous love is wrong. It is contrary to the will of God. Amnon knew it, as did everybody else in those days. The law of Moses was quite clear, and they believed in the law of Moses. But Amnon fell in love with Tamar, and he allowed that feeling to override all other considerations until it became the one ruling passion in his life.

Driven by desire for the forbidden, he cruelly raped Tamar. And then he hated her. His 'love' turned out to be a mirage, a self-deception to sophisticate a lust which once sated could no longer conceal its true identity. The love/hate goddess was well satisfied with the offering.

This wretched story contains all the essential elements of modern-day romanticism: feelings divorced from reality and truth, rebellion against what is right in the sight of God and the association of sex and violence.

Romanticism is one of the most pervasive philosophies of our generation; it is the supreme spiritual, creative and adventurous force in our teenage culture. Virtually all popular forms of art, music and literature reflect and proclaim its values. The strutting stars of pop lead the worship, popular porno authors write the devotional books, film-makers, photographers and artists provide the icons, TV personalities give their testimonies, 'experts' teach the doctrines. Multitudes follow, and the goddess is continually satisfied.

We see the fruits of this idolatry in teenage promiscuity, in sexual violence and perversion, in marital unfaithfulness, in addiction to pornographic literature, videos and films, in drug dependency, and in rebellion against authority. But it goes deeper. Romanticism is a parody of the truth. It offers excitement, adventure, passion and creative fulfilment—all the things one gets with authentic Christianity—but through service to a false god.

Why do children from Christian homes find all this so difficult to resist? We'll see a little further on.

Sensualism—the god of self-indulgence

The second is perhaps more familiar. In Philippians 3:18–19 Paul says: 'For, as I have often told you before and now say again even with tears, many live as enemies of the cross of Christ. Their destiny is destruction, their god is their stomach and their glory is in their shame. Their mind is on earthly things.'

This is what John called 'the belly god' in his book *The Healthy Alternative*. It is that tendency of human nature towards sensual indulgence without any thanksgiving to God.

It is, of course, perfectly right and good to enjoy pleasurable sensations. God made us that way. He gave us skin that feels pleasant when it's stroked. He gave us appetites that can be satisfied with food and with drink, noses to enjoy smells, eyes to behold beauty. His one requirement was that we should render thanks and worship to him as his proper due and as our proper response.

So when, for example, we enjoy a meal, we should praise the Lord. And when a husband and wife make love together, they should do the same. A satisfying piece of music should evoke thanksgiving. Rather than denying pleasure, the Christian should get more pleasure out of life than the unbeliever. In 1 Timothy 4:4-5 it says, 'For everything God created is good, and nothing is to be rejected if it is received with thanksgiving, because it is consecrated by the word of God and prayer.'

However, for the sensualist the pleasures have become an end in themselves: pure self-indulgence. There is no thanksgiving to God, no glorifying of his name for these gifts, and no moderation of desires according to the degree to which those thanks can be rendered. Appetite unlimited!

We see it so clearly in present-day consumerism. Why is it that our society demands an endless supply of consumer goods, an unlimited variety of foodstuffs, and a new model of car each year? Precisely because of the influence of this god.

Now, we're not suggesting for a moment that progress is wrong or that we shouldn't enjoy the benefits and comforts of modern technology—simply that we should beware of the deceitfulness of this god. Jesus said, 'Watch out! Be on your guard against all kinds of greed; a man's life does not consist in the abundance of his possessions' (Lk 12:15). There is something seductive in all this. Like the foolish husband intoxicated by an illicit affair, we lose sight of reality. We persuade ourselves that we need this, it's all right, we're still in control.

Just how far out of control sensualism can get, can be seen by a look at the recent history of the Western world. The eighties saw a period of almost untrammelled covetousness. People were encouraged, indeed seduced, to borrow and to spend as though there were no day of reckoning. The result was recession, negative equity, countless bad debts, bankruptcy and the creation of a deprived underclass in our society.

Falling into debt is only one symptom of losing control. There are others far worse.

Why is it that advertisers and promoters invest such enormous amounts of energy, time and money to convince us that what Jesus said isn't true? Simply because they themselves are trapped in the same circle of sensual greed. They too want to be able to indulge their appetites in the service of this god.

Teenagers are bored because they are being conned! The belly god never satisfies. However much we consume, self-gratification cannot give meaning or purpose to our lives. It can only make us feel good at the most superficial of levels, and after a while that becomes boring, if not downright irritating.

Mysticism—the god of self-worship

The theory of evolution paved the way for us to worship our own powers. Remove the idea of a Creator, observe the natural world and come to the conclusion that you are at the top of the evolutionary ladder. Learn, as never before, to manipulate nature to your own ends until you are intoxicated with your own powers. Then look for those *real* powers—the spiritual ability to control destiny, to unite with the cosmos, to realise your own godhood, to be a Universal Master! What do you have? You have the New Age movement.

It's a hotchpotch of ideas embracing everything from holistic healing to concerns over global warming. Many of the concerns are legitimate, some of the proposed remedies valuable, but the fundamental philosophy is decidedly anti-Christian. It influences our young people to believe that all the problems of the world can be solved by looking within ourselves, where instead of finding a sinful heart needing redemption, we find a repressed and underdeveloped god awaiting release and fulfilment.

The temptation to occult power is a real one for all of us, but especially for young people who often feel powerless in the face of the world. Little wonder that many find themselves drawn into mystical experimentation, with all its attendant dangers of spiritual deception and psychological damage.

Human beings need to worship. If we reject the living God, what else is there but to worship nature, and ourselves as the pinnacle of nature?

We must stand firm in our conviction that God is the Creator and Sustainer of the world, and that human beings need the forgiveness of their sins secured by Christ at Calvary. It's not a popular message because it challenges our independence and arrogance. Yet that is precisely what needs to happen if we are to be saved from deception. The cross of Christ is the only place where we discover the ultimate truth about the meaning of life.

We have got to help our children see through the lies and myths of modern society. Romanticism, sensualism and mysticism are false gods. Neither we nor they must bow down and worship them.

6
Reaction or Revelation?

Start talking to teenagers about culture and they quickly become edgy. 'What do you know about it? Are you trying to impose your antiquated values on us? The world's moved on since you were young. Leave us alone to make up our own minds.'

And they are partly right. We do react from our own prejudices. Here is an example of what we mean. John's mum never used make-up. Janet rarely uses any—John says she's too beautiful to need it, in any case! So he was quite convinced that his daughters were never going to paint their faces, let alone wear earrings when they became teenagers. Very biblical, very sound—a man of the Word, not a man of the world!

Then our daughters reached those fascinating years. Guess what they wanted? And forcibly so. To give John credit, he did a humble re-examination of his views. Was he really being biblical or was he merely prejudiced by his own upbringing, or for that matter by his personal preferences?

The result? Our beautiful daughters wear earrings and make-up!

Often we don't immediately know why we react. Some things just feel wrong. In the late sixties we used to call it 'bad vibrations'. It isn't an explanation that will satisfy today's questing children, who view such ideas of their parents as incredibly naïve. Rationalism rules when it's convenient.

Sometimes the basis of our reaction is purely a mistrust of the unfamiliar—in other words, it's a subtle form of fear. At other times it may be because, say, the music just isn't to our taste. It's perfectly valid to feel like this and it helps our kids if they can understand that it is our problem, not theirs. Trouble brews when we allow our personal reactions to be projected as though it was all their fault. That's when they feel got at.

There's a world of difference between, 'That's terrible music,' meaning, 'I don't like it,' and, 'That's terrible music,' meaning, 'You've got lousy taste,' or, 'It's evil music and you shouldn't be listening to it.' We must know the difference, and so must our children.

Of course, there are many occasions when we may be genuinely discerning something evil—the spirit of the age, romanticism, sensualism or New Age mysticism. That form of reaction is justified and we should seek to teach our children how to recognise this.

We may properly paraphrase 1 John 2:15-17, 'Do not love secular society or anything in secular society. If anyone loves secular society the love of the Father is not in him, for everything in this secular society, the lusts of the flesh, the lust of his eyes and the boasting of what he has and does comes not from the Father but from secular society. Secular society and its desires will pass away, but the man who does the will of God lives for ever.'

Pretty strong stuff. And even more so in Revelation 18 where the code word 'Babylon' represents a society, its commerce, culture and religion, passing away under the judgement of God. Little wonder then that we should react when we perceive the same spirit in our own age. It is right to do so.

When we do, however, let us make sure that we are aware of the real issues.

The heart of the matter

The prophet Isaiah seemed at one point to take quite a detailed interest in women's clothing:

> The Lord says, 'The women of Zion are haughty, walking along with outstretched necks, flirting with their eyes, tripping along with mincing steps, with ornaments jingling on their ankles. Therefore the Lord will bring sores on the heads of the women of Zion; the Lord will make their scalps bald.' In that day the Lord will snatch away their finery: the bangles and headbands and crescent necklaces, the ear-rings and bracelets and veils, the head-dresses and ankle chains and sashes, the perfume bottles and charms, the signet rings and nose rings, the fine robes and the capes and cloaks, the purses and mirrors, and the linen garments and tiaras and shawls (Is 3:16–23).

What does it mean? Why is God suddenly against necklaces, bracelets and perfume? Many times the church has read passages like this and failed to get the real point. Instead, decrees have been issued forbidding women to dress in anything other than drab. The dowdier you are, the holier you must be.

That isn't what Isaiah is getting at, however. He opposes, not the jewellery, but the attitude of heart that it reveals. The nation was socially and economically divided, and what the prophet attacked was the arrogant, glamorous display of the luxury-loving rich who showed no regard for God or for the poor.

The issue then is not about whether it is right or wrong to wear earrings, but of whether the wearing of such is part of a callous indifference to the plight of the poor. That message is tremendously relevant in a day when it is so easy to buy yet another piece of expensive fashion without even considering whether the money should be put to the benefit of someone else in need.

Here is another illustration of the importance of heart attitudes: 'You have spent enough time in the past doing what pagans choose to do—living in debauchery, lust, drunkenness, orgies, carousing and detestable idolatry' (1 Pet 4:3). The Christians in Peter's day were prepared to be thought strange because they forsook the party-loving, drunken, orgiastic, drug-taking culture to which they had formerly belonged. It was for them an issue of discipleship.

Peter's words continue to have relevance, especially to certain kinds of discos and acid house raves which our children may be invited to attend. It's legitimate to ask a Christian in such an environment, 'What's a nice girl (or guy) like you doing in a place like this?' But it doesn't follow that our children should be banned from attending all discos or parties, or that we should forbid them ever to listen to pop music. Living under grace requires that we assess each disco on its moral merits, rather than simply issuing blanket decrees from the aloofness of our armchairs.

There are Christians who feel that the only way to cope with all this is to withdraw completely. They become Exclusive Brethren, or enter monasteries, or become ascetics in the hills and deserts where separation from the world means living with only the most basic necessities of food, clothing and shelter.

Not that this is the answer. The story is told of a Christian hermit who was tempted by a band of demons.

They tried everything they could to make him sin—storms, heat, lustful visions, promises of wealth—all to no avail, for the man had truly separated himself from the world and its comforts.

Then one day the devil himself was passing by. The demons sought his advice in desperation. With a sly wink, the devil approached the hermit and whispered these words in his ear: 'Your brother has just been made Bishop of Constantinople.' It worked with fiendish success. At once, jealousy filled the hermit. Separate from society he was, but he could not separate himself from his own heart.

Evangelicals, on the whole, do not choose the path of asceticism because of their clear responsibility to witness for Christ in the midst of the everyday world. The trouble is, and our teenagers see this more clearly than we do, instead of retreating into the desert, we often retreat into the past. We kid ourselves that history sanctifies culture. The music of Beethoven, Tchaikovsky and Chopin becomes more acceptable than that of, say, David Bowie, Elton John and Madonna.

Yet society was as sinful then as it is today. Tchaikovsky was gay and Brahms was a dirty old man. Mozart's *The Magic Flute* is based upon the rites of Freemasonry. Even John Dowland's lute music was considered riotous in its time.

Or, to come more up to date, do you recall the years of rock 'n' roll? Wonderful stuff! The music of our teens. But our parents didn't think so. They were still into the dance bands of the forties and when the now-tame film *Rock Around the Clock* hit the screen they thought, quite rightly in fact, that a revolution had just begun.

The Beatles' song, 'Yellow Submarine', is now sung as a nursery rhyme in our primary schools—made safe by the years. Yet when first released, it was a song used to promote the drug culture.

The same phenomenon happens in the world of fashion. Take jeans again—though we're not obsessed with the topic. A revolution took place in women's jeans in the early sixties. Until then, most women wore a side zip variety. Then came raunchy front zip jeans for women, liberating and sexy. Christian women of the time had real problems with the fashion and the image associated with it. But not any longer. Time has sanctified jeans. The same goes for trouser suits, bikinis and so forth. Not for nothing are Evangelicals called conservative! Nor is it surprising that our teenagers consider us old-fashioned and reactionary.

Yet, up to a point, putting the clock back works. Cultural spirits do lose their power over the years. What causes sin in one generation may not do so a generation later.

The reason for this is quite simple: the spirits behind the cultural icons of our society are only sustained by men's worship. While a demon has worshippers, the idol will have power. Once replaced by something else, it loses that power and becomes just 'nice'. Hence, Satan, 'the Prince of this world', seeks continually to capture the hearts of each new generation with some novel attraction. It worries him little that the power to corrupt may be short-lived, provided he can keep the process going—and he has a pretty impressive track record so far.

It is, to our mind, a pity that Christians have not been equally zealous in producing a culture with sufficient vibrancy seriously to challenge Satan's sway. Most of what the church has come up with is either born out of a ghetto mentality or is merely a morally sterilised version of what the world does better in the first place. But how to remedy this dismal state of affairs is beyond the scope of this book.

Anxious parents want to know how to guide and protect their children through the temptations of the world that now is. Even so, it's high time the gauntlet was thrown down.

Merely reacting superficially against the world leaves us in the not-very-inspiring position of having to refuse almost everything fashionable and to live instead with Satan's cultural cast-offs. There is a better way.

True Christian discernment is concerned with the effect of things on the heart. Does my listening to this music, visiting this place, reading this book, draw me nearer to God or drive a wedge between us? Am I uplifted or depressed by the thing I give myself to? Am I provoked to give thanks or made to sin?

However, Christian discernment is also concerned with what we transmit by our behaviour. As we have seen, it's tempting for parents to retreat into the past. That tells the world that our gospel has no relevance for today. It also makes our kids feel the odd ones out among their peers for all the wrong reasons.

We would like to suggest that a better approach is to take the world as we find it, a mixture of good and bad, and use its resources so that we might become a revelation of the good news in the way that we express our culture. In the next two chapters we will look at fashion and music as two ways of illustrating how we, and our teenagers, can do this.

7
Dress to Bless

Clothes can be a real area of conflict in teenage years. Who knows how many arguments begin with, 'Do I *have* to wear this uniform?' or, 'You're not going out looking like *that*, my girl!'? Yet most of these tensions can be avoided with just a little discussion and insight. What does the Bible have to say about clothing? Is it possible for our children to dress in a manner consistent with Christianity, without looking like religious freaks?

Speaking of the behaviour of wives regarding their husbands, even those disobedient to the word, Peter writes, 'Your beauty should not come from outward adornment, such as braided hair and the wearing of gold jewellery and fine clothes. Instead, it should be that of your inner self, the unfading beauty of a gentle and quiet spirit, which is of great worth in God's sight' (1 Pet 3:3–4).

Paul writes to Timothy in similar vein: 'I also want women to dress modestly, with decency and propriety, not with braided hair or gold or pearls or expensive clothes, but with good deeds appropriate for women who profess to worship God' (1 Tim 2:9–10).

These two passages have often been interpreted in a manner which suggests that female spirituality is best demonstrated by dowdiness. If you look attractive, you must be unspiritual! The old Authorised Version translation didn't help by translating the word 'decency' as 'shamefacedness'. Hardly surprising that the world should look at some Christian women and say, 'What a shame!'

The original Greek actually carries a different meaning. It suggests that God wants you to be tidy and harmonious. He wants your clothing to be measured by good values, and by what is appropriate to the situation. A woman's inner beauty in Christ should be allowed to shine forth in the way that she dresses, so that she becomes a walking revelation of the gospel. This doesn't mean wearing T-shirts covered in texts or jackets bestrewn with badges. We're talking about the outward expression of inner values, not the religious *Yellow Pages* on legs.

Clearly the flashy glamour of the *Dynasty* or *Dallas* clothes-horses is inappropriate for Christians. And it is obviously unbecoming for a Christian woman to dress like a woman of the streets. But it is equally a bad witness for her to dress scruffily.

Jan feels strongly that mums should be good examples for their daughters to follow. They should never feel ashamed of how their mothers look, either because they're such a frightful mess or because they look like mutton dressed up as lamb. Young-looking fashions are one thing, but teenage clothes seldom go well with thirty-five-year-old faces and hips! We should look after ourselves, care for our hair, feel comfortable and at ease because we dress to suit the occasion. It doesn't take a lot of money to do so; just a sense of self-worth. And it's that which our children need to learn from us.

Teenagers need to be aware that there are modes of dress which express something quite contrary to the gospel. Blatant seductiveness is one of these. Particularly at party-times we should encourage our girls to check on the message their clothes might be transmitting. Girls from

Christian homes can be surprisingly unaware of the impact that they might have on non-Christians at a school disco, simply because most of their social life takes place in the relatively innocent confines of the church youth club.

If seductiveness is inappropriate for Christians, so too is depressiveness. Take a trip into, say, Brighton at any time of day during college term and you'll see large numbers of students dressed in black. Many of them will be expressing the anti-gospel fashion called Goth. Goth philosophy is obsessed with death and alienation. Its view of life is essentially cynical. Christians, by contrast, are gripped by hope. Accepted in Christ and looking for his coming kingdom, we face the evils of the world with a bright determination to do something about it. Funeral shrouds do not become us.

Aside from the veto against men dressing up as women (or vice versa), recorded in Deuteronomy 22:5, the Bible has little to say about men's fashion. This may mean we shouldn't say too much either. However, clothes are to do with image, and image is a communication of what we are, or what we want people to think we are. And that's where radical Christian values come in.

So we may legitimately question whether our sons should opt for, say, the Rambo-style of clothing which suggests violence and revenge. Similarly, bovver boots and shorn heads, or studded leather and chains convey a message of anger against society. Male earrings have associations with romanticism and homosexuality in particular. It's right that as parents we should discuss with our sons whether these are the images they really want to communicate, or whether they have just become caught up in a current trend.

Sometimes maintaining a Christian value system does visibly set us apart from those around us. That can be difficult for a young teenager, and we must be sensitive to the fact. We do our boys no favours if, for example, we insist that dressing as a Christian means wearing a scaled-down version of Dad's clothes. There's no reason why a Christian lad shouldn't look 'cool' and dress with style. Fortunately, just now there is no difficulty in obtaining fashionable clothes which our sons can wear with pride to express manly Christian virtues. Let's encourage them to do so.

One way of seeking to become a revelation of Christ in our clothing is to be guided by the fruit of the Spirit. For instance, a girl may decide, 'Well, today I'm going to dress to demonstrate the peace (or joy) of God,' or, 'This week I want to communicate the love of God in the way I clothe myself,' or, 'My style will be restrained today because I'm going to show the self-control of the Holy Spirit in my life.'

In other words, we should try to communicate some of the values of who we are. It is helpful to look at ourselves and ask, 'What comes through of my character today?' We may find that we have styles for long seasons which express the dominant characteristics of God's work in us. You may have a child who is naturally very joyful and flamboyant. Well, that can be the joy of the Holy Spirit. He or she may love to dress in bright colours. That's not contrary to the word of God. That is expressing the joy of God.

Be ready for anything, however. Your child might just turn up looking like a rainbow, hair included, with the defence that they're just reflecting God's covenant today.

Approaching the subject this way is far better than just conforming to the in fashions of the media-manipulated world—let alone falling for the New Age legalism of personal colour coding and the like. Let us encourage our children to discover what best expresses themselves in Christ.

To do this they will need freedom to experiment, as well as good advice. Letting them know when they have got it right is far more constructive than criticising them when they make a mistake. Many a foolish parent has ruined a child's day by telling them they look awful, just as they are leaving the front door and it's too late to do anything about it. We can all afford to live for a while with garish hairstyles and make-up experiments that didn't quite come off. It's part of the fun of growing up.

And let them be a revelation of themselves in Christ, not of us. We must allow our teenagers the room to find and express their own Christian identity. They have different faces to us; they have different characters. And remember, they're of a different age!

8

The Singer and the Song

Here is another subject fraught with potential for domestic nuclear escalation. Music makes the heart glad; it can also drive the parents mad.

Music is one of the most powerfully uniting forces in the world. For that reason, it is also one of the most divisive. Attack teenagers' musical tastes and you attack their culture and their generation. For it is the medium through which they express their ideas and values—just as we did in our own youth. You may wonder how, but their music gives them comfort and security. Woe to you if you seek to disturb it!

But disturb it you will, if only to prevent your eardrums rupturing. High volume seems to be part of the very nature of some pop music. It doesn't really work if it's played quietly. At least, that's what they tell you. Nevertheless, you have a reasonable case to insist that you shouldn't have to listen to their music if you don't want to, any more than they should be obliged to listen to yours.

Decibel levels can be controlled by regular reminders—and there are always the headphones if everything else fails. However, it is worth pointing out that listening to music through earphones at high volume can permanently impair your child's hearing.

The kind of music they listen to is another matter altogether, and one that needs to be handled with wisdom.

Many Christian parents have serious misgivings about the entire rock scene. This isn't helped by stories of the Lord's Prayer being recited backwards by so-called satanic groups, and the like. (Believe it corrupts if you want to, but it seems to us that to say things backwards is childish rather than sinister. There are more subtle dangers elsewhere.)

It is easy to denounce the whole scene, switch on the latest Spring-Hosanna-Stoneleigh-Kingdom-Harvest-Restored-Frontier-Festival Bible Week worship tape, and insist that's all there is to it. None of this promiscuous rock rubbish. Songs of Zion alone shall grace our ears in this home!

Musical taste is highly subjective. It is also age-sensitive. However much we try, most of us will still find ourselves more at home with the music of our own youth than with the music our children now listen to. That in itself is enough reason for us to avoid over-hasty judgements on their preferences. Here are a few other factors to take into consideration before we pull the plug on their ghetto-blasters.

Music and moods

The environment in which it is played strongly conditions the impact of a piece of music. For example, let's say you enjoy brass band music. It's fine on the seafront promenade, but if an Adolf Hitler uses that same music to stir up his fanatics at a Nazi rally, your appreciation may decline dramatically.

Or you may come across a piece that sounds like a cat caught in a meat-grinder, only to find that the same music expresses perfectly the anguish you feel when the newscaster reports on a series of harrowing atrocities taking place in one of the world's trouble spots.

Images and associations change the feel of music. Ravel's *Bolero* is a passionate composition in its own right, but few would have considered it as music for making love to, until it was used for that purpose in the widely-watched film *10*. Thanks to the advertisers, the *largo* theme from Dvorak's *Symphony No. 9* triggers images of nostalgic Northern industrial towns and Hovis bread. Yet nothing could have been further from the composer's mind as he so eloquently expressed his love for the new world of North America.

It isn't possible then morally to categorise music apart from the culture and usage of that music. And, as we saw with 'Yellow Submarine', that usage may change from heavy drug scene to nursery class over a relatively short period of time.

It's a point worth making to our kids. 'Wot's wrong wiv listening to "Bend my mind, bend my body"? I fink it's good music,' may need the reply, 'Perhaps. But would you really want to sit down and listen to a group of gays trying to get you to join them, if they were just talking and not singing?' One of the great powers of music is its ability to draw us in. The Pied Piper still plays his tune. He may lead children to the mouth of the pit. Some fall in.

If music can carry a message because of its associations, it can also reinforce or change the mood we are in. 'Listen, they're playing our tune, darling!' is a reminder of the happy days of our courtship. Similarly a piece of music may recall a painful, broken relationship. Kids can easily associate particular tracks and albums with good times or bad times in their experience and use that music either to reflect what they feel or to change their present feelings. Instead of criticising, we may do well to listen to what they are playing and so understand better what is going on in their lives.

Natural noises

James 1:17 says, 'Every good and perfect gift is from above, coming down from the Father of the heavenly lights, who does not change like shifting shadows.' There is no such thing as an implicitly holy musical style. All melody, rhythm and harmony is from God. It's how these are combined and used by man that determines the music's potential for good or evil.

It is no surprise to find that many of the modern worship songs that bless people across the world have rock rhythms. Lots are written by musicians whose styles were formed by the Beatles era. Yet those same rhythms can be used to promote sex and violence.

Many Christians would like to believe that the created world provides us with 'natural' sounds (by which they mean sweet and quiet) that should form the basis for our music. You know the sort of thing: the sound of soft winds, the cooing of the dove and the somnolent lapping of the waves on the seashore. This view expresses more a sentimental desire for peace and quiet than a real understanding of 'natural' music.

When we first moved to our home in Hailsham, we were treated to the full repertoire of a song thrush every day, beginning at about three o'clock in the morning. The music was lovely, the programme timing appalling. It did little to soothe our sleep, 'natural' though it was.

But God has other kinds of music in creation. He has his own heavy metal bands that slam the senses with a veritable wall of sound and drown out all other perceptions. The Niagara Falls have that effect, so does a full-blooded July thunderstorm over the South Downs. The Bible says that the sound of the saints when they're worshipping is like the sound of many waters; like the roar, the overwhelming ear-blasting, mind-numbing thunder of a gigantic waterfall—heavy metal, if you like.

God has his summer seashore rhythms, but he also has his rattling rains and clattering branches. He has his screechings. The wind can be the gentle breeze of God's soul, but have you ever listened to that howling, whistling, weird and macabre winter's gale? It's all part of God's infinitely varied music.

Different music, like the varying moods of nature, blesses in different ways at different times. John finds it very difficult to work with earphones on and rock music pounding in the middle of his brain—it doesn't help his sermon preparation! But there are times when he has sat in traffic jams in the centre of London and turned Radio One up full blast, and that has brought peace and order into his life. It's his way of fighting back against the discordant jangle of city traffic. Our children do their homework quite happily with the same music. It's their way of fighting back against the discordant jangle of their overstretched brains.

Lyrics and lifestyles

Ah, but what about the words? Some are quite disgusting; others promote rebellion and anger. Most are fairly neutral and simply reflect a modern teenager's view of the world around. These lyrics are helpful because they are assisting our children to articulate what they really feel about life. That may not be what we would like them to feel, but it may have a lot more reality than our idealised, orthodox Christianity.

Of course, much of the time they're not really listening

to the words anyway. That can be a safety factor; it can also lead to a subtle indoctrination, and we should certainly teach our children to be aware of what they're listening to. We should encourage them to avoid profane lyrics and those that engender destructive moods into their souls.

The vulnerable are most at risk. Those without values, or those in rebellion against your values, can be affected. But kids with otherwise well-balanced lives will see most rock music as just entertainment, or even education as to what their peers are thinking. After all, it's worth remembering that acid rock did not lead most of us into the drug culture in the early seventies any more than most of us become Freemasons by listening to *The Magic Flute*. Evil the world may be, but God and his providential goodness are far more powerful.

If we sometimes have problems with types of music, we may also find that the lifestyles of many composers and performers are not to our taste either. To a point, that no more disqualifies a piece of good music than the lifestyle of your milkman disqualifies the milk he delivers. Sinners are quite capable of drawing on God's providential goodness.

The difference between the music and a bottle of milk, however, is that milk merely nourishes our bodies. Music affects our personalities and our values. We cannot entirely divorce modern rock from the lifestyle of the performer and indeed the visual imagery that goes with the rock video. It is a fact that much modern music is blatant propaganda for immoral and dissolute living, often exemplified in the performer's own lifestyle. Young and impressionable teenagers, caught up with the excitement of life, are easily conditioned into accepting anti-Christian values. Rock music can be very sensual; it fits well with a promiscuous age, and it'll do our children no harm to be aware of that fact.

Music, like wallpaper, is subjective. It is to do with the effect that it has on us. And that provides a key to assessing the rightness or otherwise of a piece of music. Can you give thanks to God for it? First Timothy 4:4–5 says: 'Everything God created is good, and nothing is to be rejected if it is received with thanksgiving, because it is consecrated by the word of God and prayer.'

If our children can honestly thank God for their music, it's OK—at least, for them. We may not be able to do the same ourselves. That's fine. All it then needs is a little mutual understanding about volume controls.

9
Money, Money, Money

As the song says, 'It's a rich man's world.' Money can't buy you happiness, but it can reduce the misery to very tolerable levels. Bombarded as we are by endless advertising, borrowing schemes and promises of total fulfilment through owning the latest gadget or taking expensive holidays, it's not surprising that money is a source of contention between parents and their teenage children.

How much pocket-money?

This is a perennial vexed question for which there is no simple answer. A lot depends upon where you live and what your own standard of living—and that of your neighbours—is like. What would be excess for one child would be poverty for another. However, there are certain principles to help us.

What can you sensibly afford?

Within reason it does teenage children good to know at least something about the family finances. This is necessary education for their future.

Obviously, we have to exercise care, otherwise they might start discussing our personal business with their school friends, with all manner of undesirable consequences. Likewise, by their own budget standards, we might appear incredibly wealthy. It helps to show them where the money goes, so that they can see how little is left at the end of the monthly distribution. If you are struggling financially, you must be careful not to lay that particular burden upon your child. Some sensitive children can feel guilty as a result and may want to give you all their life savings. It sounds wonderful, but you shouldn't take advantage of them. Others will be distracted with a worry they can do nothing about.

Handled positively, this exercise will assist your children to understand the economic bracket life has saddled them with. It stops them making unfair comparisons with other families who, apparently, own Jaguars, Rolls Royces and Range Rovers by the dozen, and never think twice about giving their kids £50 in small change to tide them over until Saturday.

What are their necessities?

We parents have to decide what we are giving pocket-money for. This needs discussing with your teenager. For example, do you expect your child to purchase school dinners and pay for his travel to and from school? Is the allowance meant to cover buying their own clothes? Are you expecting your daughter to purchase her own sanitary requirements? Or do you provide simply leisure money?

There are no hard and fast rules. Those who provide a full allowance give their children a high degree of responsibility in handling their own affairs, but there are pitfalls, particularly for young teens. What seems a large sum of money to them may lead them into a fool's paradise. They can easily be seduced by advertising and, before you know it, might have spent all their money on something quite wasteful. You will then have to bail them out.

There is also the risk that your child might be robbed. So, if you do decide to operate full allowances, teach your child not to carry large sums on his person. Flashing a few notes around is an act of bravado that can end in grief.

Many parents opt for providing travel and lunch money, and pay for their children's clothes directly. This has the merit of keeping a control on what they wear.

How much is needed for social dignity?

There is no doubt that too much, or too little, money is harmful for children. What we are after is a happy medium—moderation in all things. The ideal way of finding out what this is, would be to ask the parents of your child's peers and then for all of you to agree the same figure. However, this is rarely possible—though we have known church groups to achieve a fair degree of unanimity.

The best most of us can do is to sit down with our child and discuss the cost of a reasonable social life. This might include subs for the youth club, money for the leisure centre, the purchase of a few sweets and a snack or two at a fast-food bar and a little spare for giving and for savings, for example.

It is probably better to lean on the side of caution and make extra gifts from time to time, rather than to be too lavish on the weekly allowances, only to regret the consequences.

Prices rise, and our children's needs become more sophisticated as they grow older. This means raising their allowances from time to time, and maybe changing the way we handle such matters as the purchase of their own clothes.

Part-time jobs

Traditionally, children have supplemented their pocket-money by doing paper rounds, taking Saturday jobs or working a few hours for the local fast-food chain. It has to be said straightaway that generally the money is poor. However, it does teach children the dignity of earning their way in life, and it also gives them useful work experience that may help when they come to look for full-time employment.

There are certain disadvantages. Paper rounds, if combined with a lot of evening activities, can leave teenagers exhausted so that their school work suffers. Saturday jobs make it almost impossible to enjoy a full social life, particularly when it comes to summer outings or regular sports fixtures. These considerations need to be talked through.

We should also ensure that our children are not working for unscrupulous employers. We have come across numerous situations where teenagers working for food chain stores have been badly treated, swindled and put at risk through a failure of the local managers to enforce health and safety laws. Children also need to be made wise to the possibility of sexual harassment.

Some parents prefer to give their children a bit more pocket-money in exchange for doing jobs around the home. It has certain advantages over the above. However, it can be difficult to enforce standards, and maybe we should encourage our children to pull their weight in the home without the enticement of financial reward.

Financial services

If you want to make real money, trade with other people's! That must surely be the motto of the finance and investment houses which make such vast profits even in times of recession.

Recent years have seen the targeting of teenagers by banks and financial institutions. Today they are offered free accounts, credit cards and loans at an ever younger age. There is obviously money in it. People tend to settle for the bank they first choose. But the real money is made on the exorbitant interest rates and service charges that are applied to the various forms of credit accounts.

We had best prepare our children. Some will be wiser than we are and will work the system to their best advantage, playing off one building society against another, keeping free bank accounts while there are no charges and then switching if charges are applied. Other children are not so astute and may find themselves in difficulties.

Student loans

You don't get something for nothing. Because of government cuts in student grants, there is an increasing pressure on students to borrow money cheaply. This is all well and good until the time comes to repay the debt. At this point, the student may find that the rate of interest has now soared above the normal level and he is faced with a crippling burden in the early years of paid employment (assuming he can get a job) that makes the prospect of marriage, or property purchase, virtually impossible.

It is difficult for teenagers to see even two or three years ahead, so it is best to advise them to avoid student loans like the plague. Remember, borrowed money is always easier to spend than money you have saved up by your own hard efforts.

Credit cards and charge cards

We have a simple rule concerning the use of credit cards: if you cannot pay off the bill in full every month, you are not gifted to have a card. Destroy it.

We have counselled countless teenagers who have fallen prey to the in-store charge card. 'Buy now, pay later' means precisely that. But who thinks of the paying at the time of purchase? Least of all the immature. Who realises that once you start buying on credit, you can no longer afford to save up to buy with cash, simply because you are paying around 20-25% interest on the repayments? It is no exaggeration to say that some people doom themselves to a lifetime of debt and to a lower standard of living than they might otherwise have had simply because they borrowed heavily in their late teens. The recommendation is simple: if you want it, save up for it. If you can't afford cash, then don't buy it.

Budgeting

When we were children our parents used to put money in jam-jars on the mantelpiece. Each jam-jar was labelled with a particular household bill. This was how many in our parents' generation avoided debt. It isn't wise or easy, however, to do this in an age of electronic money. Instead we have to do our budgeting on paper.

Keeping accounts is a necessity in the modern world and we should begin to educate our children by showing them how to manage a simple balance sheet for their pocket-money. If they have a bank account or building society passbook, they should make sure all the figures tally. This practice will be a godsend for them in adult years when they have to manage their own household accounts.

Giving

You will doubtless have your own views on giving to the church and to charity. This may or may not be in accord with the teaching of the Bible, but we hope that you have at least taught your children to be givers. It reminds them that we are tenants on this earth, and not owners. We should share the good things we have received and not simply spend everything on ourselves. There are also many powerful divine promises that apply particularly to those who tithe their income to God.

Because many people are victims of the current economic system and long for financial liberation, we have written a book on the subject called *Handling Your Money* (Word). It will prove helpful reading for your teenagers and will show them how to avoid the pitfalls.

10
Discernment

The sea of history is littered with islands once inhabited by those who thought it possible for Christians to live entirely separate from the surrounding waters of secular culture. Each in its turn has been deserted and all that remains is ruined edifices and follies. That sea is also littered with the corpses and wrecks of those who drifted unthinkingly with the tide of public opinion; a tide that seduced them fatally onto quicksands, treacherous reefs and the cruel coastlines of spiritual compromise.

Dotted here and there, however, are fine craft in full sail. The fair breeze of the Spirit drives these boats. Their masters steer a skilful course with the confidence born of good instruction and learned experience, for they know the whereabouts of the deep water channels, and how to avoid the rocks and treacherous tides.

It is possible to isolate ourselves from the world; it's very easy to drift unthinkingly with the tide of popular opinion. But God wants us to do neither. Faced with the challenge of our culture, he wants us instead to exercise true spiritual discernment. In other words, we must learn how to distinguish good from evil. Hebrews 5:14 tells us that this is the mark of the mature person—hence, a worthy goal for us parents.

Discernment develops as we learn how to apply the

Scriptures to the issues which confront our daily lives. This is of particular importance when it comes to facing those subjects and situations upon which the Bible does not pronounce specifically. That is when we need to have a good grasp of spiritual principles.

Here are one or two examples of what we mean. In Philippians 4:8 Paul writes, 'Whatever is pure, whatever is lovely, whatever is admirable...think about such things.'

That is helpful advice in an age of cynicism. Today's teenagers are led to doubt whether there is anything truly good. It's fashionable to attack 'nice' things. Satire of the *Spitting Image* type is very popular. Aerosol graffiti defaces attractive monuments. Sick humour, sordid titbits and tales of violence constitute much popular reading matter and locker-room conversation. The tabloid press feeds on scandal.

This emphasis on baseness lowers people's self-esteem. It discourages aspiration and instead fosters failure, mediocrity and indifference. You don't have to be a very acute observer of the British way of life to see that this is a national disease.

Anyone can knock down the achievements of the past; few people can recreate them. Virtue is easier criticised than copied. Those who wish to build their lives successfully will fail in the attempt if they only study the demolition jobs on others.

We must help our children to see through this prevailing mentality. They must discern these negative attitudes for what they are—and reject them in favour of something better. Teach your children that goodness is 'cool'. Encourage them to nobler values than those of their non-Christian friends around them. Help them to appreciate good things and not to be afraid to have genuine heroes and personal aspirations.

First Corinthians 6:12 provides another helpful principle for discernment. Here Paul is dealing with a catch-phrase that was doing the rounds. 'I'm old enough to do what I like. There's no harm in it. Everything is permissible to me.' The apostle nods sagely and replies, 'Sure. But not everything's beneficial, is it?'

He goes further. 'Everything may be permissible to me (it's legal, isn't it?), but I won't allow myself to be mastered by anything.' This is a useful argument when it comes to, say, smoking or other popular drug-taking. Nowhere does the Bible condemn tobacco, marijuana or cocaine as such, so it is quite permissible for Christians to smoke and still go to heaven (you might get there a bit quicker, actually). But it most certainly isn't beneficial. It masters you. So the Christian says, 'I could do it, but I choose not to, because it is unhelpful and I'm not going to let anything like that take away my freedom.'

Paul applies this principle in the realm of sexual morality. People were saying, 'The stomach's for food, and food for the stomach. You feel like sex—have it.' But God never intended that the body should be used for immorality. To do so is to abuse God's purpose. Therefore, it's unacceptable for Christians to be immoral. It's a bit like using a telephone handset as a hammer. Something gets broken.

Is it all right for a Christian to go to the disco? Nowhere does the Bible say, 'Thou shalt not go to the disco!' But will that particular disco be beneficial? Will it enhance our freedom in Christ and enable us to keep our bodies for the use God intended, or otherwise? Let your teenagers judge it for themselves.

What kinds of magazines and books should they read? Where do they go on holiday, and who with? What are acceptable videos? The same principle of discernment applies. There's a lot of muck in the world, and we have to be careful not to put our foot in it.

What should they do about alcohol? There are many Christians today who feel it is appropriate and part of their freedom in Christ to drink moderate amounts of alcohol. There are many for whom that would be deadly dangerous. Our children have to find out for themselves what is freedom for their lives, and what is bondage. We must not lay upon them a legalistic anti-drinking attitude or a legalistic drinking attitude. They must discern for themselves. It is, after all, just as legalistic to say, 'Thou shalt drink,' as to say, 'Thou shalt not drink.'

Christian discernment challenges the roots of both religious legalism and the permissive bondage of the secular world. It is based upon grace, but not cheap grace. What we are suggesting isn't a licence for our kids to do as they please, but a way of giving them real strength and responsibility when it comes to taking on the pressures of the world around them. It's teaching their eyes to see.

This all takes time, and we may have to be patient while they work it out. We have met Christian punks with bright orange Mohican haircuts, half a dozen earrings in their ears, pins stuck through their noses, dressed completely in black, pounding their brains out with heavy rock. Now, we don't think they yet understand how to manifest the Spirit of Christ through their lifestyle. They have adopted something else for want of discerning anything better. They're God's confused children. But the confusions pass and eventually they begin, in most cases, to see that the only really radical way of life is to be a disciple of Jesus Christ.

Pray we must, worry we will, attack we mustn't. Confrontation does have its place, but far less so than we think. There are often wiser ways of correcting their extremes.

Many years ago, the teenagers went through a fashion phase in our then church. It was for hot pants. John never spoke from the pulpit to condemn it. Instead, we encouraged folk to joke about it. The result? The girls who were participating in the craze saw the funny side of it, realised it was a somewhat inappropriate fashion for church, and dropped it. If John had ranted from the pulpit about gleaming, provocative thighs, it would probably have invoked the wrong reaction. The girls would either have stopped coming or have felt they had to score a point. For to be sure, they were not deliberately dressing to seduce the deacons! A breath of gentle humour often has more power than a fierce trumpet blast.

So, these things need sensitive handling. Do let them have some fun. Great powers may operate behind society, but our children are better insulated than we think. Let us not drive them into extremes of over-reaction or self-rejection by condemning everything they try. Instead, let us encourage them to live by grace and so discover with thankfulness all the good gifts of God which will make their lives worth living to the full.

More homework

What irritates or worries you about your child's lifestyle? Talk it through with your teenager as one who wishes to learn how he ticks. Don't confront him, but enquire.

Ask your child to imagine he is you. Would he approve or disapprove of the things that worry you? Ask him why, and seek to learn from his answers something of his outlook on life.

Part Three

Love, Sex and Mirages

11
The Mother of Harlots

We cannot avoid her, this gross, scarlet Mother of Harlots, presiding with cynical lust over the affairs of men. Babylon the Great. City without Shame. Her blasphemies and adulteries pollute the whole earth.

Today, with the explosion of information technology, there is no escape from this Babylonian culture that we call 'the world'. Newspapers, magazines, videos, radio and television ensure the encounter takes place—not in pagan temples, but in the sanctity of our own homes. The choice is plain: let Babylon into your lives or lose touch with what is happening in the real world. Only those who wish to withdraw totally can hope to remain unaffected by its all-pervasive influence.

Escapism, however, is not a valid option for our teenage children—or for us parents. So we must take on the world; and in no area of life is the ensuing conflict of values more real than in the realm of sexual beliefs and practices.

For the past four decades, the Mother of Harlots has revelled in promoting the indulgence of everything that is sexually perverse and decadent. As a result, we raise our children in a society which is more confused sexually than probably any previous generation.

Are they homosexual or heterosexual, or something in between? Should they sleep around? Do condoms really protect you from AIDS? Who wants 'safe sex' anyway? Masturbation is good for you, but pornography is sexist. Unless you're a woman—then female erotica is liberating. But what's the difference? Both forms of literature are aimed unambiguously at the groin and both are exploitative. Sex before marriage is apparently essential in order to find out if you are compatible. But why marry at all? Unwanted babies can be killed before they're born, but child abusers should be brought to book. Why this inconsistency?

John expressed something of the current confusion in a recent poem.

>Ah, little girl so sweet,
>Play innocent in the street;
>You'll grow up soon;
>And then they'll teach you what to do.
>
>Who are you?
>A female form
>Designed for men;
>But why?
>A woman's touch is far more kind.
>
>Let us open up your mind,
>Explore the taboos of the past;
>Be not afraid;
>For God is dead.
>At last!
>
>And your friend,
>The little boy;
>He'll grow up, too.
>Confused,
>Uncertain who he is;
>He must not be a chauvinist!

Perhaps he's gay?
Many are;
Or so they say.
Find out;
Come out; cry out.
The church won't mind;
It rather likes the other kind!

But hedge your bets,
You might be straight.
Just as well to copulate
With those of other sex than you.

Leisure, pleasure,
Lots of fun;
Sex is good for everyone.
Condoms keep you safe from AIDS,
And all the other nasty things
That give promiscuous sex a sting.

At least,
That's what the experts say;
And no one's taught
A better way!

It's tempting to press the panic button at this point. How are our children to cope with all this? What can we do to protect them? It appears a daunting task and one from which we may well wish to flee.

But better to face the foe than to pretend the foe doesn't exist. And that, sadly, is the trouble with many Christian parents. Sex is a taboo subject, a constant source of embarrassment to them. So much so that some are too embarrassed even to admit that they are embarrassed. It's an attitude which is no help to our children. Ostriches may know a lot about sand, but they are poor guides for crossing the desert.

A young man approached John at a teenagers' conference with this typical cry: 'I'm in a terrible mess. If you saw me at home, I'm a good Christian boy, but on the inside I'm a sex maniac. But I can't talk to my parents about it.'

There was nothing abnormal about this lad. He certainly wasn't a sex maniac. But he was wrestling with normal teenage desires in a world that had plunged him into a personal battle between his Christian beliefs and the provocations of Babylon. He felt ill-equipped to fight it. The real tragedy was his inability to communicate the problem to his parents—and that was mostly their fault.

This embarrassed silence, this implication that sex is impolite and unclean, can have devastating effects. A young woman from a good Christian home may optimistically enter into marriage, only to find that she is sexually frigid because of an unconscious shame engendered by her parents' negative attitudes. It could ruin the marriage.

The opposite can also happen. A church leader's daughter gets pregnant by her boyfriend. Why? Because she rebelled against her parents' prudery and lack of understanding. Or a son becomes a wild donkey at college because he doesn't want the patently inhibited sex life he perceives his parents to have.

However difficult we may find it, we must face the issues square on with our kids. They need intelligent guidance from us if they are to find their way through the sexual minefield.

Secular society has been far from afraid to talk about the subject. Books, television documentaries, sex education lessons, magazines, all ensure that no aspect of human sexual behaviour is left untouched. As a result, our children probably know more than we do about the facts of life.

Unfortunately, what the world does so well, it also does so unrighteously. Sex is taught as something you do when you fancy it, like eating ice cream or going to the pictures. Most modern sex education is divorced from Christian ideas of chastity, covenant love and marital faithfulness. Technique has replaced trust, contraception is more important than commitment, satisfying the libido substitutes for sustaining love.

And this is no accident. Those who influence the ideas and practices of men and women in society have quite deliberately rejected the Christian way. In fact, most sex education today is based upon the assumption that the church (and therefore God) is the cause of all the trouble in the past, and true liberation is found by positively rejecting its standards.

Root of rebellion

All modern secular sexual values have sprung from a root of rebellion against the will of God. This is especially true concerning the ideas of chastity before marriage and of faithfulness within marriage.

Four ideas are promoted to make this rebellion sound intelligent and advanced. It'll help us in guiding our children if we know a little bit about them.

God messes you up

In the late fifties and early sixties the ideas of the psychologist Sigmund Freud became very popular. He taught that the root cause of much of the stress in our lives is due to an unhealthy restraint on our latent sexual desires. This is caused by a repressive conscience called 'the superego', which was created by the taboos imposed on us as children by our parents, society and the church. This superego is in direct conflict with our libido, or primeval sex drive. The result is inner tension which expresses itself in neurotic behaviour.

The average reader may be forgiven for concluding from this that too much self-restraint is supposed to send you barmy. Freud had a point, of course. A society in which people are not allowed to express their emotions or to talk about their deep feelings will produce some very uptight individuals. But it is quite another thing to imply that chastity, self-control and fidelity are a sign of being sexually neurotic. Overnight the virtues have become the vices and *vice versa*.

The proposed remedy for all this was to throw off the restraints of the superego and thus give vent to all our basic animal desires. Hence, it is now healthy to masturbate, to sleep together out of wedlock, and to lust after your neighbour's partner. Purity is sick, and so are those who teach it.

We once had in our church a woman who attempted suicide. Fortunately, we were able to save her life, but the hospital put her under a psychiatrist. He counselled her thus: 'The reason you attempted suicide—the cause of all your problems—is your church and your religion. What you need to do is stop attending these church meetings, go down the pub, pick up a lad or two, get laid a few times and you'll feel much better.' Pure popular Freudianism. Thankfully the girl in question refused the counsel and sought God instead.

Monkey business

There was a time when, if we wanted to understand mankind, we looked to the best we had produced. We studied the lives of saints and heroes, of great thinkers and leaders. It was their characters which challenged and inspired us to attain our full humanity. But that has all changed. Nowadays, we go instead to the zoo and watch the behaviour of the chimpanzees at their tea party.

Once we believed we were made in the image of God; now we are merely monkeys who have evolved out of their fur. Instead of looking up for inspiration, we look down for explanation. The body language of apes, especially their rituals of courtship and copulation, debunks all the mystery and magic of human love. Morality is a myth, religion a rip-off. Primates of the world, unite—you have nothing to lose but your souls.

It's not true, of course. Fortunately, God keeps enough artists, poets and saints in the world to remind us otherwise. But the pervasive myth flourishes to justify the morals of alley-cats among those first created in the image of God.

Apparently, we can do as we please. Since animals cannot be held morally responsible, any form of sexual behaviour is permissible. In this human zoo men are supposed always to be randy and women permanently on heat. Like animals, they may play the courtship ritual and copulate all they like, when and with whom they like.

The resultant anguish is appalling: guilt, pain, confusion, shame, use and abuse, mistrust and hatred. 'Why, O why do I feel like this if I'm only a naked ape?' We've had a society that has tried to live like animals and then found it got hurt like humans.

Rock on, baby!

In a previous section we took a brief look at romanticism—that philosophy which is at once exciting and adventurous, but seeks the thrills of life in the forbidden, the perverse and the rebellious.

Lady Chatterley's Lover opened the avenue for exploring these realms in popular literature. Rock music has played a significant part in directing juvenile eroticism along the same paths rather than those of sexual fulfilment in marriage. Rock music isn't wrong; nor for that matter is eroticism. It's the ends to which they are presently directed that cause all the problems.

Because music is so much a part of our teenage culture, the sexual message is easily received. Until Christians gain a greater influence in the rock industry, romanticism will hold sway, immorality will continue to be glorified in passionate song, and multitudes of young people will keep up the pretence that it's great. Make no mistake, romanticism's false fires of love and sacrifice but thinly conceal the ashes of lust and death.

Love is all you need

The fourth factor is a semi-religious one. Remember the Beatles' song 'All you need is love'? That song popularised a theology which went something like this: in the past we had rigid laws dictating our conduct. Today we have the option of total licence—do as you please. But that is obviously fraught with difficulties. Is there another way, some middle ground, something we can cling to in the absence of any absolute standards?

The answer was apparently to be found in the Bible— 'Love is the fulfilment of the law' (Rom 13:10). All you need is love. Provided what you do is loving, then you don't have to worry about any absolute laws. Love preserves you from going down the path of total licence and at the same time gives you the flexibility to meet any situation without recourse to rigid rules.

It sounds very fine at first sight. But if we set love over against absolute standards, we finish up making God's commands the enemies of true love. Instead of love being the correct heart attitude with which to fulfil the law, it fast becomes the alternative to law—a lawless love, no less.

In fact, what happened was that the *feeling* of love became an absolute law in its own right. Hence, when parents complained of their children's immoral behaviour, they were met with the apparently unarguable response, 'But we're in love!'

When the noble, sacrificial love of God is reduced to the pleasure principle, anything goes. In the French pornographic novel, *L'Histoire d'O*, the central character is abused in every manner conceivable and accepts it all willingly because *l'amour*, 'love', is absolute. Even sexual violence becomes defensible with the plaintive cry, 'But I love you!'

When these four ideas first came on the scene, people believed that sex was the greatest thing on earth. It was love. Today's young people are still taught this, but cynicism is setting in. They're finding that the permissive path is not all it's cracked up to be. In fact, it's proving to be full of pitfalls and potholes. Since the advent of AIDS you can even die from sex.

The sex act has become for many a charade, a pretence at enjoyment, something that everyone is expected to do during their teens. Gone is even the thrill of rebellion.

One of the sad effects of all this is that it is now estimated that some 30% of young people who get married stop having sexual relationships within six to nine months of marriage. Thinking they have found love through sex, they enter marriage on that basis, only to find that this isn't the way life works. Boredom, disappointment and disillusionment set in—people give up on the greatest pleasure that God has granted the human race.

That, of course, creates tremendous tensions and

pressures in the marriage. The disappointed are always tempted to see if the grass is greener on the other side of the fence. Abstinence is fertile soil for adultery.

It has to be said that some kind of rebellion in the realm of sex was justified. The world of the forties and fifties was repressed and legalistic in many ways. Typical of the attitudes was a Christian book which did the rounds in our teenage years. It warned of the sins of young men wearing bathing trunks on the beach and exposing their bared chests. The veto was enforced—it has to be said dishonestly (though there is some small risk)—with dire warnings of skin cancer to those who insisted on persisting with this flagrant display of flesh. Goodness knows what the author would have made of today's topless fashions!

More seriously, many people suffered needless anguish and heartache because of the prevailing hush-hush attitudes. Those who needed help couldn't get it. Frustration was rife, ignorance commonplace. But what was needed was not a rebellion against morality, but a revolution into God's true freedom. The latter has been a long time coming.

12

Practise What You Preach

There is an important prophecy in Jeremiah 31:29 concerning the Incarnation and the coming of the kingdom of God: 'In those days people will no longer say, "The fathers have eaten sour grapes, and the children's teeth are set on edge."'

A time is coming when people will take responsibility for their own sins, says Jeremiah. No longer will they excuse themselves by blaming their parents. Indeed, God will form a New Covenant, and the people of that covenant will delight in heart obedience to his laws.

The prophecy offers great hope for us anxious parents. Why should our teenagers and young adults have their teeth set on edge any longer because of the sexual sour grapes eaten by the previous generation? It is surely time for the people of the New Covenant to set about rearing a generation for whom love and sex are sweet and beautiful, and where bitterness in relationships becomes a thing of the past.

Whether this happens or not will depend to a large extent upon us. We want to suggest that there are three things that we can do to help our children make a success of their sex lives.

Keep your own house in order

No man is an island. 'Free love' is very costly—and not just to the participants. The sins of the fathers (and mothers) are visited upon their children. Painful it may be, unfair it may seem, but that's one of the realities of life.

The first step in helping our children live sexually pure lives is that we do so ourselves. We must practise what we preach.

Past sins need resolving. You may yourself have been immoral. Hopefully, you have repented of the deeds. But sexual sins have a habit of lasting long in the memory. Feelings of guilt may arise every time we recall the acts of which we are now ashamed. If only we could start again! But it's too late. What's done is done. And we may fear that, in spite of all our efforts, the same things will happen to our children.

The gospel never minimises sin, or its consequences, but it does provide a remedy that is totally effective. The blood of Jesus cleanses us from all wrongdoing, and that includes sexual transgression. Jesus deals with both the guilt and the feelings of uncleanness that accompany sin. Sobered by our past we may be, but there is no need for us to wallow for ever in our shame. Rather, we ought to glory in the redeeming power of the cross of our Lord Jesus Christ.

True repentance is always worth it. Not only is it the key to saving our own souls, but it contains the power to break the curse on our families. Iniquity doesn't have to pass from one generation to another, for God shows mercy to the thousands who love him. Part of what it means to be a new creation in Christ Jesus is to give your family a fresh start, free from the consequences of past sins.

If the past is taken care of, what of the present? Tragically, wrecked marriages litter the church because good Spirit-filled Christians somehow think they're immune from all sexual temptations and find to their cost that they're not. They fall into sin. Take care, for 'if you think you are standing firm, be careful that you don't fall!' (1 Cor 10:12).

Check . . .

. . . that you are free from adultery, and, if you are a single parent, from the temptation to satisfy loneliness by lust. Coveting another person's partner still causes more marital break-up than any other single issue.

. . . that your heart is clear about homosexuality. In spite of the fudging of the issue by some church leaders and the blatant defence of the practice by the 'gay Christian' lobby, the Scriptures make it quite plain that the practising homosexual (male or female) does not have eternal life, any more than does the practising thief, liar or adulterer.

. . . that you have dealt with the issues of pornography and lustful masturbation. Jesus said that if your eye or hand causes you to sin then you should deal drastically with it. Better that than go to hell (Mt 5:27-30).

. . . that you have faced the issue of incest squarely. There is nothing more damaging to a child than to have been party to an incestuous relationship with a father or mother. It constitutes one of the most fundamental betrayals of trust in human relationships. Be on your guard against temptation, especially as your children enter their adolescent years.

Those are the negatives and it is a sad commentary on the state of the church that we find it necessary to write this, but hard pastoral experience has taught us the need to do so.

Let your love shine

Now to something positive! The greatest help we can be to our children lies in us providing a role model of what loving relationships are all about. It's not enough that we tell our kids, 'Mummy and Daddy love each other.' They must see it demonstrated.

Love is a learned experience. It can't be taught from a book. Life experience teaches children whether they are loved or not. It also instructs them as to whether their parents really love one another.

Many children worry about this, particularly in a society where marital breakdown is rife. Rows between parents, simmering tensions and the like, hint that the family may fall apart. And with that goes the child's own sense of security.

We are being watched! Teenage years especially are a time of acute observation. What they see and hear and feel profoundly affects our children. They need first-hand experience of that parental role model which we call 'a passionate covenant'.

True marriage is, after all, not just a piece of paper. It is a bonding of hearts and lives in passionate love so that two people can call themselves one flesh for life. The will of God is nothing less, and that's what our children must see if they're going to believe that Christian marriage works.

Part of what this means is that parents should not be secretive or embarrassed about the sexual side of their relationship. We're not implying that you should embarrass your children by doing things in front of them that properly belong in the bedroom. However, they need to know that you make love and enjoy it—and there are plenty of signs of physical affection which can be shared in their presence, all of which say without words that love is real and love lasts.

In a healthy family, children are secure in the aura of the love their parents have for each other. And this is not simply an ethereal, spiritual love, but one that permeates right down to the essential earthiness of the marriage bed.

Teenagers get to know if you are sexually satisfied. Acutely aware of the subject these days, they sense signs of frigidity or frustration. This doesn't mean you have to walk into breakfast with your arms around each other, saying in a loud voice, 'Wow, didn't we have a great time in bed last night, darling? Isn't it wonderful that we both orgasmed together—just like we always do?' It's enough to make your kids choke on their cornflakes.

If it's going well, you won't need to say so. And if things could be better, why not read our book *A Touch of Love* (Kingsway, 1986) for a complete guide to sexual fulfilment in the will of God? Even if you've been married for a number of years, it can bring great refreshment to your relationship.

Make the subject open season

This is the third thing we can do. Sex education should have begun from the very first time they asked questions about where babies come from. With our own children we told them everything in blow-by-blow detail. It bored them silly. They were not the least bit interested and usually they started playing with their toys after about two minutes. Fascination came later.

We thought it was better to tell them the truth when they were young rather than make up gooseberry bush stories that we would have to undo at a future date. Growing up with a knowledge of the subject that was as natural as anything else in life, there have never been really embarrassing moments, nor have we had to cope with the disinformation given out by schools. We got in first.

Even so, as children reach their teens (and even earlier with girls) there comes the time for that much-dreaded talk about the birds and the bees. Of course, if the subject is already familiar it will not be too embarrassing. Even so, expect some difficulty. Children at this age are self-conscious themselves. Their bodies are changing, as are their feelings also. The moment needs choosing with wisdom.

We suggest going outside somewhere. Go for a walk. Holidays are a good time. Begin the conversation casually, something along these lines: 'Hey, son, you're looking good these days. I suppose it's time we chatted a bit about growing up.'

On the whole, mothers find it easier to talk to their daughters than fathers to their sons. This is because mothers usually have the practical issue of periods to start the talk off. Fathers don't have that in the same way. They may be needing instead to talk about nocturnal emissions and masturbation. These are more difficult subjects to open up on. But it must be done. We owe it to our sons. Far better we talk openly than simply sling a book at them, saying, 'Read that! Talk to me if you have any questions.' Because they won't.

If you're a single parent, you may be feeling cheesed off by now, because we're writing about mums and dads, and you're just feeling the pain of your own situation. What are you to do?

A single woman can obviously talk to her own daughters, but what about if she has sons? They need to hear from a man. This is where the church comes in. The point of having brothers in Christ is not that they become substitute sexless husbands, but that as real brothers they help in the areas which need a man's input. Choose someone who is securely married, whose wife you get on well with, and who has a rapport with your son. It is best if he has sons of his own. If you have no one else, then talk to the youth leader, minister or elder. Ask, 'Will you chat with my son, please? To be honest, I can't handle it, and somebody needs to.'

Having opened up the subject, we have to keep it open. One talk doesn't do it all. That doesn't mean becoming obsessive about it, but as children progress through their teenage years, their perceptions and needs change. We must respond intelligently and sensitively to them. There are several ways in which we can do this.

13
Keep Sex on the Agenda

Keeping the subject of sex and sexuality open means taking advantage of the natural opportunities that arise.

Body beautiful

For example, it is important that we acknowledge our children's maturing bodies and flatter them on their physical development. By this we mean expressing a genuine appreciation of their emerging adult figures. Needless to say, although the subject has its humorous side, we should avoid any kind of crudity—there's enough of that going around in the world as it is. We should also refrain from embarrassing our children in front of others. Most kids do not appreciate being greeted by Aunt Ethel with the words, 'Ooh, hasn't he *grown*!'

We all worry about how we look, and never more so than in those uncertain teenage years. Our task is to encourage self-confidence in our children. Better that Dad assures his daughter of her emerging beauty than for her to have to wait until she is desperate for a fellow to do so at any price.

Now, there obviously comes a time when girls need somebody else other than their fathers to tell them they're lovely. But if with cuddles and kind words you have reassured them that they are wanted and loved, when they do enter a relationship with a fellow it will be because they really want to, not because they are driven by insecurity and the need for physical acceptance.

One of the real problems we face today is that girls in particular are bombarded by the media with a message that tells them they do not look good. The not-very-subtle way this is done is by confronting them with ultra-glamorous models and pop stars who, for an absolute fortune spent on clothes, body shops, makeovers and diets, can appear like goddesses.

The aim is to make your daughter feel ugly by comparison, unless—and here's the point—she spends a similar small fortune attempting to look like the model. No wonder many girls just have to buy new clothes every week and that hardly-used make-ups, hair dyes and fashion flops litter their rooms. That this hasn't happened to the same degree with guys is simply because the media hasn't worked so thoroughly on male style—but it's coming.

Tell your daughter she does look all right. God didn't get the plans screwed up when he made her. Things may look too big, too small, too long, too short, too fat, too thin. That's not the issue. God made her like that and somebody's going to love her the way she is. Out there, somewhere, is a fellow who is tuned to just her shape. Never mind her response, 'Good grief, if he's looking for this shape, what kind of shape is *he* going to be in?'

Boys need equal encouragement. They want their muscles admired. 'Feel that bicep, Dad. Go on. It's harder than yours.' (It probably is.) They want to know that you appreciate their manly chests and the hairs growing on their legs—and, of course, that carefully cultured adolescent moustache. You'll have to get used to regular arm-wrestling as well. Eventually he will beat you at it—he's determined to try, anyway. Even Mum will have to go through the charade of taking on young Mr Universe.

Style is 'in' for boys. They want to look cool, not scruffy. What Mum thinks matters, because she is first representative of the female sex. If she's not impressed, will the girl down the road be? Boys want Mum's opinion and her encouragement, but they don't take kindly to nagging. So Mum has to take on the role of a female admirer and offer just a touch of advice here and there to improve the already dazzling image of the cool dude. Call it male ego-enhancement if you like; we'd sooner call it the ministry of encouragement!

The question of homosexuality

This seems a good point to pass some comment on the issue of homosexuality. It's certainly a subject that will be discussed at school and we will be wise to talk about it at home.

Recent years have seen a concerted challenge mounted against the traditional Christian view which says that homosexuality is a perversion of God's intentions. Today it is being justified in schools and in the media as a valid option for young men. Even the AIDS crisis, which was introduced into Western society largely because of homosexual practices, has not deterred those who would push for positive discrimination in favour of homosexual orientation.

Although recent legislation has helped curb this to some degree, it is an unavoidable issue for our children, particularly with the lowering of the age of consent to eighteen in Britain. Because of the confusion and undoubted threat, we want to suggest how to protect our kids from within.

Straightaway, we must say that there is no serious evidence to suggest that homosexual orientation is genetic. Children are not 'born that way'. That is not to deny that we all have hereditary traits. Clearly we do. And one of these may be a certain effeminacy. However, though the girlish young man may find himself a particular target for homosexual attention, it is a fallacy to equate male effeminacy with homosexuality—just as it is foolish to suggest that masculine-featured women are lesbians.

The main factor that influences a child towards a sexual preference for his or her own kind is the lack of a proper parental role model. Hence, 'inner protection' for our children depends upon getting this right.

For example, one classic syndrome for inducing homosexual desires in a boy is that of the dominant mother and weak father. In a home where a bossy woman rules the roost while the father refuses to accept his God-given headship role, a young boy soon learns that women are a threat to his own male identity. He has only to observe the emasculation of his browbeaten father, constantly harassed and in retreat, to be left with the increasing suspicion that women can hurt him, too.

He observes the emotional blackmail, experiences the histrionics, notes the lack of physical affection. As he grows up, he reacts. He may respond aggressively and become chauvinistic, even violent towards women. He may choose relationships with weak women in order to dominate them. Or, he may feel so utterly inadequate to form a relationship with a woman, that he turns to the company of men for his sexual satisfaction.

How important it is to observe and implement God's order for husband/wife relationships in the family. How essential for our children to see us demonstrating our affection for one another. It's here, above all, that they learn the naturalness, the beauty and the fun, the security and fulfilment of heterosexual love.

The other common factor in producing male homosexual orientation is the absence or inadequate provision of a father. Deprivation of fatherly love and attention is always a bad thing for children. It is particularly bad for boys during the period of life around puberty onset and for a year or two beyond.

At this time, a natural process occurs for which we have recoined the term 'homophilia'—love of the same. It means the child develops an affection for his or her own sex, though the child would not recognise this as sexual, nor is it appropriate to credit such an embryonic phase with overt sexual desire.

The dynamics are very simple: the child is evolving into a sexually aware adolescent. The release of hormones, the physical change, forces the child to find a new identity.

Psychological identity does not come about in a vacuum. It is largely formed out of relationships with others. Hence, during that insecure phase the child will look initially to those of the same kind as himself—one reason why hero worship is so common at this age. The hero may be a pop star, a teacher, a youth leader—best of all the child's father. If he is there.

In a healthy family, a wise father will handle the homophilia stage. A secure son will express considerable affection, and indeed physical affection, for his father at this age. This may appear to the father to contain a sexual element, which can be disturbing. But all that is happening is that the child is discovering what it feels like to be a man. He is irradiating himself with adult masculinity. In a very short while the process will be completed and the adolescent boy will emerge as a fully-fledged heterosexual. He may then turn his attentions briefly to his mother before looking outwards to the lush plains of girls unlimited.

Similarly, a daughter will develop a homophilic relationship with her mother before, perhaps, falling temporarily 'in love' with her father as a threshold stage to adult relationships with men. This is a vulnerable time of life. Fathers and mothers in their turn, while responding to their child's need for more than usual, quasi-sexual attention, must beware of falling into any kind of incest. Sadly, this happens all too often in our decadent society. Similarly, established homosexuals may take advantage of the child and draw him into sexual activity. Either way, the results will be nigh on disastrous.

There is another very evil possibility. It is that those with sinister motives may take advantage of this phase and teach that a child who feels an affinity with the same sex should consider himself or herself homosexually orientated, at the least bi-sexual, and therefore free to engage in homosexual activity. The pubescent child, knowing that these feelings are taking place and not being given any other explanation for them, is then faced with the possibility of being gay.

This knowledge can be traumatic in the extreme. Guilt, shame, self-revulsion on the one hand; ruinous homosexual experimentation on the other. All based upon a falsehood. Little wonder Jesus said, 'Woe to those who cause these young ones to stumble.' What should be an emergence into sexual security becomes a permanent identity crisis.

Dad needs to be around. The father always away on business, too tired to talk and irritated by his son's demand for physical attention when he is there, does a grave disservice to his offspring. Mum needs to be around. If she is always too busy with her career, the housework, the

Women's Institute, the bingo or the church fête, her daughter will be left wondering about her own essential identity as a woman.

Our children's well-being is more important than our jobs, our church activities, or our leisure interests. If we do not sacrifice our convenience, we may well sacrifice their entire lives. Manliness is propagated by our presence; it is communicated by our gestures and our speech; it is observed in our activities. Our boys find their masculinity in the intimacy of our aura. No one else is good enough to provide this, and we betray our sons if we ourselves fail to do so. It is no less true with regard to mums and their daughters.

There is another major area in which fathers are absent today. It is in the single-parent family where Mum (usually) has custody of the children and Dad is either dead or otherwise gone from the scene. We are painfully aware of the ache that this produces in the hearts of these mothers. 'Where am I going to find the man who can be a role model for my son? Will he be at the mercy of the unscrupulous? Will he never find his sexuality?'

This is a genuine problem. Many from single-parent families do grow up sexually confused. It is one of the tragedies of a permissive society. However, there is real hope and it is to be found in the body of Christ, provided we rise to the challenge. God sets the solitary in families (Ps 68:6). We are convinced that as a practical expression of our true faith, every single-parent family should know a measure of adoption into a two-parent family in our churches. That this should be done voluntarily and with real pastoral wisdom goes without saying. But it is an effective way of facing the reality of the lack of a parent and goes some way to compensate for it.

Children without a father still need fathering. If the way

isn't open for a younger widow or divorcee to remarry, then brothers in Christ need, in all purity, to go some way to fulfilling that adult role model.

It does not follow from all this that children from a dominant mother/weak father family or children with an absent father are automatically going to grow up homosexually inclined, any more than everyone catches a flu virus when it is doing the rounds. Life is more complex than that and there are many random factors which come into the picture. However, just as we can take measures to reduce the likelihood of us catching the flu, so we can take steps to provide our children with the emotional and spiritual health they need in these morally infectious days.

Girls often have a higher level of physical contact with other girls than do boys in our society. This doesn't mean your daughter is a latent lesbian! Established homosexuality between women is far more likely to originate as a result of maltreatment by men than through the frivolity of friendship going too far. Even so, if a same-sex friendship is becoming too exclusive, a quiet word may be in order.

Confident virgins

Another way of keeping sexuality on the family agenda is to pick up on the attitudes that are going around the school, college or workplace when you are talking to your children. Sex is a regular topic of conversation, not always of polite conversation, in the world. Ask your children what their friends think about homosexuality or divorce—or virginity.

It is quite possible that your child is the only self-confessed virgin in the class. (There will be others, but they'll never dare admit it.) It can be a lonely role. Ask them how they cope. It will provide you with the opportunity to boost their confidence.

In times past, virginity was prized because it meant that a woman wasn't pregnant with someone else's child when she got married. In the last thirty years, virginity has become a teenage complaint akin to acne—something you want to get rid of as soon as possible. But things are changing.

Encourage your kids that nowadays virginity is something to be prized again. It is no cause for shame. To be a virgin (male or female) means you are virtually guaranteed free from syphilis, gonorrhoea, genital herpes, non-specific urethritis, genital warts, crab lice and AIDS. It's not in fact true that everybody is at risk from the latter. If your kids are virgins and they marry virgins, they are virtually immune from the AIDS epidemic. The only people at real risk from this disease are the promiscuous and drug abusers. (In this country, blood products are now screened to prevent transmission by transfusion. There is some small risk to those involved in the medical and associated professions.)

Of course, there are plenty of other good reasons for remaining a virgin until you are married. Better a new car than a much-used old banger, and so forth. Build up your children's confidence. Chastity makes sense. Sleeping around is stupid.

Masturbation

Secular wisdom has reacted against the heavy condemnations and hypocrisy of the past by saying that masturbation is not only permissible, but is thoroughly good for you. We parents need to get our own thinking straight if we are to help our children in this vexed area.

The entire direct teaching on the subject in the Bible can be summed up in one word: nothing. Nowhere does it say that the practice is sinful. What it does condemn is the sin of lust. If masturbation takes place with lust, and realistically it often does, then that combination is wrong in the sight of God.

However, we must be careful when we talk about this subject not to make our kids feel that even lustful masturbation is the worst sin under the sun. It's not. People are far more likely to go to hell for respectable sins like pride, self-righteousness, slander and envy than ever they are for masturbation. At least this practice tends to make folk feel rotten, with the potential for repentance, which is more than can generally be said for the others.

The subject needs sensitive handling. Angry confrontation is not the answer. On the whole, we should teach them that it is an unhelpful practice to indulge in. Self-control is a better way. Give them practical advice about avoiding situations in which they might be particularly vulnerable. This may be along the lines of not lying in bed for all of Saturday mornings, or spending too long in the loo. Your advice needs to include other ways of dealing with depression than by resorting to self-comfort. For boys in particular (both girls and boys are encouraged to masturbate these days), using up their excess energy in sports activity is an important aspect of sexual self-rule.

Find an opportunity to discuss pornography with your children. What's wrong with pornography? It debases women (and men too in hard porn). It treats women as less than human. It turns real people into two-dimensional fantasy images, reducing them to mere sex objects.

God made women in his image. There is, therefore, in every woman that which is Godlike. Pornography reduces people to the level of animal functions. It debases the noble image of God.

You may come across a pornographic magazine under your son's bed, or an erotic novel in your daughter's bag. You might even come in unexpectedly one evening to find your children watching a steamy 18-rated video. What are you going to do about it?

Wild outbursts seldom achieve anything useful. The fact that the item was hidden in the first place suggests they already feel a certain sense of guilt. To come in heavy may only increase that to the point where in self-defence they argue a case which they don't really believe in. Most porn is viewed initially either out of curiosity (and let's face it, we are all insatiably curious about sex) or momentary weakness—or even for a laugh.

It requires quiet, rational discussion, encouragement to remain pure, and a clear reaffirmation of your wish not to have this material in the house. You can then help them burn or otherwise dispose of the offending items.

Perhaps we should add here that our own reading and viewing habits should set a good example. Check your bookshelves. Are you happy for your children to read any and all of your books? Is your newspaper more to do with page-three boobs than world events? What do they find you watching on TV?

Having said all this, we must still avoid unreality. We do no favours to our children if we refuse to acknowledge the presence of lust in this world, or if we are unwilling to discuss sexual matters with them in a very down-to-earth and explicit manner. Much modern literature, for example, is not sexually exploitative but nevertheless explores frankly the sexual complexities and realities of human relationships. It may be perfectly legitimate for your children to study such literature for their GCSE examinations.

There's another point to be made, too. There is a world of difference between lustful looks and 'girl-watching', or for that matter 'boy-watching'. Many Christian men in particular have been in false bondage over this, feeling that to notice a pretty girl is to fall immediately into the sin of lust.

Yet God made her attractive, so why not notice her, and give thanks to the Lord? Of course, we can be tempted to lust, and that must be resisted. Some women go out of their way to be noticed in a purely sexual manner, but a studied look at the face of the latter is usually enough to dispel lustful desires!

At a more prosaic level, your young teenagers will look at the opposite sex. Boys will sometimes spend time sitting on fences just looking at girls. Meanwhile, girls will sit in the intimate confines of the café glancing and giggling together over some hunk waiting in the checkout queue. And why not? If our children never notice the opposite sex, they'll never marry. We must not rear them to think that they can only glance surreptitiously out of the corner of their eyes in the hope that you haven't noticed. God created the opposite sex. The Bible speaks unashamedly about human beauty and sexual attraction. It also warns about the sin of lust. Our job is to teach our children how, in the words of Paul, to 'test everything. Hold on to the good. Avoid every kind of evil' (1 Thess 5:21-22).

14
Going Together

The distant peals of wedding bells were sounding in our household when we wrote the first edition of this book. Since then, all three of our children have married and already we are twice over grandparents—even though we feel hardly old enough to qualify!

Each of our children chose fine Christian partners; all were virgins on their wedding days. It was not a matter of mere good fortune. We feel our prayers have been answered. God has honoured the principles that we taught our children, and that we continue to teach teenagers in our youth groups.

We are well aware that it could have been very different. The Christian world is littered with the wrecks of ruined courtships and even broken marriages. There exists great confusion over boy/girl relationships in the church at large—far more so than in the world. Young people's fellowships regularly self-destruct because of fickle relationships, sexual competitiveness and the broken-heartedness that ensues. What can we do about it? What advice shall we give to our children?

The Christian problem ultimately revolves around one issue: we believe sex belongs only within the bounds of marriage. The non-Christian, on the other hand, usually believes that sex is for when you feel you are ready for it—

and that is probably long before marriage. Hence, most unbelievers have no real moral qualms about exploring relationships sexually outside wedlock.

This means that most relationships among unbelievers involve heavy petting early on and, in many cases, intercourse at the first opportunity—the classic one-night stand is still the Saturday night goal for many young people. The French call it *liaison sans lendemain*—a relationship without tomorrow. Very sad, when you think about it.

Serious relationships among non-Christians usually include sex before marriage (if marriage takes place at all). It's worth noting that the world has replaced the specific, real promises of the marriage covenant with the undefined phrase, 'We are committed,' to justify their sinful practices.

When Christians go out together, because of their desire to obey God and not have intercourse outside wedlock, they must play things much cooler. It is, after all, abject folly to stoke up the fire only to pour a bucket of cold water over it just as it's getting cosy.

There are really only two choices. Either we must go for totally chaperoned relationships—hardly workable these days—or we must exercise some form of self-chaperoning. In which case we need some guidelines which we can pass on to our children. You may find our own approach helpful. It goes something like this.

Volume control or graphic equaliser?

Most non-Christian relationships resemble the volume control on your stereo. You switch on and straightaway turn up the volume fairly loud—petting is soon quite heavy. Before long it's full volume and the couple are having intercourse (or some form of 'safe sex' that involves orgasm).

Many Christian young people adopt the same approach, except that they start the volume lower and don't want it to reach full volume until they are married. The trouble is, just when they think they've got it right, somebody walks by with a ghetto blaster blaring out and their volume seems far too tame by comparison. So they turn it up a bit.

Their ears become adjusted to the new noise level, and soon it goes up a bit more. Before they know it, they are engaged in quite heavy petting and may find themselves on the brink of having intercourse—the very thing they set out not to do.

The volume control approach to going together is too relative and undefined. It provides insufficient guidelines. A better approach is to plan a relationship to resemble the bands of a graphic equaliser.

As you probably know, the graphic equaliser is a means of splitting the tone control into several adjustable frequency bands. Each control covers a different range. Let us imagine that our graphic equaliser resembles five different levels of relationship, each one of them having sufficient range to allow a relationship to grow until moving on to the next one.

Band one—Fellowship

A church shouldn't be run as though it were a nunnery or a monastery. It is healthy for teenage boys and girls to meet so that they can worship, serve and play as a group. We need young people's fellowships where there is lots going on; not just Sunday morning Bible studies and religious events, but plenty of activities where they can enjoy being friends together.

To our mind it's unfair and unhelpful of parents to keep

their children in a church where there are no other teenagers. It may be fine for the parents, but the children are being denied Christian fellowship among their peers. Ultimately, without anything better being provided, they may opt for the world and in the process lose their faith.

In this 'fellowship band' let us encourage the value of singleness. The Bible has quite a lot to say about it. For instance, in 1 Corinthians 7:32-34, Paul says:

> I would like you to be free from concern. An unmarried man is concerned about the Lord's affairs—how he can please the Lord. But a married man is concerned about the affairs of this world—how he can please his wife [pay the bills, manage the kids, comfort her, etc]—and his interests are divided. An unmarried woman or virgin is concerned about the Lord's affairs: Her aim is to be devoted to the Lord in both body and spirit. But a married woman is concerned about the affairs of this world—how she can please her husband [wash his socks, cook him a meal, make the beds, etc].

What Paul is saying is that there is a vocation in life called singleness. Unmarried teenagers are in that vocation, at least for the present. There is no need for it to be a time of frustration or disappointment. It can be a period of life during which we have undivided and totally fulfilled interests in the Lord. Let's scotch the myth that the only way to find true happiness in life is with somebody of the opposite sex. It is just not true.

Jesus proved that it is possible to have an absolutely fulfilled life as a single person. The apostle Paul elected, probably as a widower, to remain single for Jesus. Many very fulfilled young people take the same line. Chastity is good. Serving God with all one's energy, including the sexual energy, is a great way of life. It doesn't need the complication of short-lived and often hurtful courtships.

Band two—Special friends

One of the great merits of belonging to a Christian group is that young people have the opportunity to know others at leisure and in a social context, without any pressure to get closer. At least it should be that way in a healthy church. If everyone who walks in is automatically paired off by the rest, then much of that fellowship will be lost.

We say this because the next band of relationship is to do with forming a special friendship with someone of the opposite sex. We are not speaking here of going out together as young lovers, but of genuine friendship. Many groups are so lacking in understanding of this that immediately a boy and a girl start even talking together the pressure is on for them to pair off. As a consequence, many are pushed into relationships they were never looking for, while others feel forced to keep their distance and so lose out on the opportunity for friendship.

To have a special friend of the opposite sex is to say that you enjoy their company and their interests, but you are no more exclusive in that relationship than you would be with someone of the same sex. The same goes for the level of physical contact. This is a relationship of friends, not lovers, and hence the level of physical contact should be no more than would be expressed to brothers or sisters in Christ.

Special friends do things together and talk together, because they like each other and share common interests or outlooks on life. It is possible to have several specific friends of the other sex, some of whom may become friends of a future spouse as well and so last a lifetime. The important point is to agree that these relationships are no more than that.

Band three—Going out together

One of these friendships may develop into love. Hopefully, by the time it does, the couple will be old enough for a serious relationship and could at least contemplate the possibility of marriage. It's not necessary or a good idea to go out with someone like this in one's early teens.

If the couple sense the relationship is changing, and one of the signs is that they both do, then they need to make a definite decision to 'move bands'. Falling in love is a very wonderful and spontaneous thing, but it doesn't take away our ability to think about what we are doing. By consciously deciding now to go out together, they keep the relationship secure.

What has happened is that they now want to be together, not just because they are friends, but precisely because they are of the opposite sex. This is the beginning of sexual love.

This level of relationship is obviously more intimate—and more physical—but we still need to recognise where it's at. The level of physical contact should be no more than that which is affectionate and therefore suitable for expressing in public. Anything which is overtly arousing is out. God gave sexual arousal as a prelude to intercourse, not as a way of saying goodnight.

This is the time for long walks and much talking; for romantic meals; for sharing the discovery of young love. It isn't a licence for heavy petting. In fact, that will hinder the development of love, and build in problems for later.

Band four—Engagement

If a couple have entered responsibly into the previous level of relationship, it is highly likely that they will want to marry. There comes a time when they realise they cannot live without each other. They have fallen deeply and permanently in love. They know each other really well. Circumstances are such that they can now contemplate marriage in the not-too-distant future. It's time to pop the question and become engaged.

Engagement is a promise to make a promise. It is a commitment to get married. To our mind, engagements shouldn't last too long. This is the home straight, the time necessary to make all the wedding arrangements. A ring isn't just a reserved notice to keep others off. In any case, long engagements significantly add to the sexual pressures. Although these may increase, couples should still be encouraged to keep themselves for the wedding night. They don't want to spoil it when they are so close to marriage.

Band five—Into marriage

All being well, then, our young people will marry somebody they have come to know in a wider context; someone who is now their best friend, a person they have fallen passionately in love with, who has already made a commitment to them, so that come the wedding day they make their vows with absolute joy and conviction. Then they live happily ever after. At least, they have a good start, a firm foundation, which will enable them to build a successful marriage. The rest is a long story and not for this book.

The most neglected band in all this is the second—special friendship. So often it is overlooked because we have copied the secular idea that the only relationship possible with the opposite sex is, in fact, a sexual one.

But if youngsters go straight into a band three relationship, and especially if they allow their physical relationship to be sexually arousing, they make a commitment greater than either of them are ready for. When the light dawns and it breaks up, both parties get very hurt. More young people leave churches through broken relationships than for any other reason.

There are other consequences. Churches are close communities. If everyone in the young people's fellowship 'does the rounds' and petting is heavy, to put it bluntly, it results in a lot of shop-soiled goods. Can God really be happy with a situation in which the bride and groom have been physically too intimate with half the guests at the wedding? We think not.

There is also the occasional embarrassing pregnancy to think of. Christians don't as a rule take precautions, because they never intend to have intercourse. If they did, it would be a commitment to premeditated sin. Guess who's most likely to fall accidentally—the Christian or the worldly-wise non-Christian?

What we're trying to show by all this is that it's possible to delay sexual awakening and at the same time enjoy the company of the opposite sex. Our model also provides a good way of ensuring successful marriages.

Whether you like our particular analogy or not, we think it important that you give your children some kind of framework for relationships. Besides what we've already written, we would also advise kids not to go out with non-Christian boyfriends or girlfriends, ie band three relationships. The reason is simple: the Bible teaches that we are not to be unequally yoked with unbelievers (2 Cor 6:14). To go out seriously with an unbeliever is to set yourself on a pathway which will lead to a costly disobedience.

Sometimes the unbeliever is converted, but more often than not it's the believer who loses his or her faith. It's best to advise our kids to look for a good, Spirit-filled Christian with whom to share this most important aspect of their lives.

One of the things that has struck us in talking to Christian teenagers is how ignorant they are about sexual arousal. Most agree that sex before marriage is out, but few seem to have any idea about how far they should go.

In our book *A Touch of Love* we use the illustration of a fast-flowing river leading to a waterfall to describe the process of sexual arousal and intercourse. Our advice is that those not intending to have intercourse shouldn't let themselves get caught in the current. There is a divinely given point of no return.

This means teaching our children what is or isn't sexually arousing. It doesn't mean they can have no physical contact. We suggest in the book that there are plenty of calm bywaters along this river. These represent the expression of sexual affection—the sort of thing you can do in public without embarrassing anyone. Let us guide our children into knowing the difference.

True love

All this may sound rather organised and far removed from the soaring passions of the romantic novels. Can we expect our inexperienced children to act so responsibly when all their school friends are pairing off at the Saturday night disco? How can they know if they're in love? Is it something you can control anyway? What did you do when you were their age?

One of our daughters had her first proposal of marriage when she was twelve years of age. We hadn't even got to the volume control, let alone the graphic equaliser by then. Sometimes you just have to handle matters gently but firmly. Young teenagers still get the feelings we used to call 'calf-love'. It's as irrational as ever it was—but we must insist that it's not true love. That may involve a bit of painful confrontation, loud protestation and angry tearfulness. Stick with it, long-suffering parent! You were like that once.

When they get older, the question becomes more serious. If your children are believers, then they will be praying for a life partner of God's choice. How do they know it's true love, the real thing, God's will for their lives?

Are they true friends? As a married couple, we are each other's best friend. We share common interests from different perspectives—*very* different perspectives! We disagree as friends do; we argue like friends; we make up like friends. That was how it was when we were courting. Marriage is more than that, of course, but it's an important part of our relationship.

If your children do not have a tested friendship, then they don't have a good basis for marriage. That's one of the reasons why we should encourage them to get to know their partner very well, both in a social context and as a special friend, before entering a serious courtship.

It's no use marrying someone you don't like. We had a guy come to us once, saying: 'I'm getting married in a few weeks' time and I've got a real problem. I think the girl I'm marrying is really ugly.'

It seemed somewhat late in the day for him to make this disconcerting discovery. We did all we could to help him appreciate her good points. Believing that the real person shines through the eyes, John suggested the fellow concentrate upon that part of her anatomy. To no avail. He replied that she was cross-eyed!

If only they had been friends. You never consider your friend ugly, even if he has a face like a plate of stew. He's your friend! What spiritual nonsense it is to say, 'Cor, you aren't half ugly, but God said I've got to love you!'

Is there true romance in your child's relationship? We believe in it. (John likes Janet to buy him roses and chocolates!) Seriously, does this fellow treat your daughter with real affection? Is he obviously caring for her? 'As now, so then' is very true in marriage. What takes place in courtship carries on. The person you marry is the person you marry, and although we all hope to improve as our relationships deepen, we remain essentially the same kind of people we set out as. If he's not a gentleman now, he probably never will be.

Make sure that the girl respects your son. Is she really concerned about him? Does she encourage him? Is she the sort of girl who is prepared to follow his lead, or does she have him in tow? In spite of all the talk about women's changing roles these days, is she going to create a good home? That doesn't mean she has to be a *cordon bleu* cook, just that she has the right sort of outlook on the domestic scene.

The essence of Christian love is sacrifice. When Paul wrote his marvellous piece on marriage in Ephesians 5 he said in effect, 'Husband lay down your life for your wife, just as Jesus laid down his life for the church.' He also instructed wives to sacrifice—to submit—to their husbands as to the Lord.

That is the nature of God's love. It is sacrificial. Is there the potential for mutual sacrifice in this intended marriage? Is there a love that puts itself out? Is there a love that is prepared to serve the other person?

These are the kinds of questions that test whether this is the love of a lifetime. They require honest answers.

Having said all this, none of us can guarantee that our children will get it right first go. Following the pattern of relationships that we've suggested above will make it more than likely that they will, but you can't be one hundred per cent sure when it comes to love.

Your child may in all sincerity enter a relationship prayerfully and thoughtfully, only to find that it doesn't work out. What are you to do? Do you remember the lifeboat illustration we used early on in this book? You must go to the rescue.

As the old song says, 'Breaking up is so very hard to do.' There will be tears and heartache, but better now than when it's too late and they've committed themselves to marriage. That would be a disaster.

All parents have a measure of anxiety about their children's future, especially concerning marriage. As Christian parents we must pray that God will not only keep our children pure, but that he will also lead them to a partner of his choice. Happily, there is a multitude of testimonies to demonstrate that he does hear the cries of his children in this matter.

We live in a world where Babylon, that Mother of Harlots, is spreading a foul poison throughout the sexual lives of this generation. We must help our kids to understand the society in which they live. Our lives must demonstrate a godly alternative. By faith we can provide an antidote for the poison and raise sexually healthy teenagers.

The devil hates it. We may wonder why the attack has been so sexually orientated. It is because the devil loathes the idea of blessing being passed from one generation to another. Every time that happens his own day of reckoning looms nearer.

Christian marriages produce Christian families. The number of the elect increases. (Not only by this means, of course. Many others come to the Lord through primary evangelism.) The return of the Lord is hastened, and with it the final destruction of Satan.

Little wonder he seeks to warp sexuality, to wreck marriages and to destroy children. That's why we have to be steadfast in our faith—understanding his methods and overcoming him by the word of God and by our prayers.

Yet more homework

If you have not yet had a genuinely honest, open talk with your children about the birds and the bees, then you should do so.

Even if you have, try discussing our views with them. You, and they, may disagree with some points. That doesn't matter too much. The important thing is that you are talking.

Part Four

Accidents, Addictions and Academic Agonies

15
Testing Times

By now you will have realised that raising teenagers isn't all plain sailing. The world is full of pitfalls for the unwary. As if that in itself wasn't enough to cope with, there are times when real disasters occur on top of everything else. These can leave us reeling, if for no other reason, because we don't expect them to happen to our children and so are ill-prepared for the outcome. We hope some of what we write here may help those who find themselves going through deep waters.

Looking back, it was no more than a slight flutter in the spiritual atmosphere, a whiff of unease that indicated something was wrong. But the police phone call was unmistakable. 'Mr Houghton? I'm afraid there's been an accident, sir. It's your son.'

In an instant your life changes irrevocably. Your plans, your diary, your evening meal—all is forgotten, unimportant. I move in a strange equilibrium between the electrified poles of mind-numbing shock and torturing panic as I climb into the car. Drive carefully, don't lose your self-control, I urge myself. I pray as I drive the eight miles to the hospital, muster the spiritual resources, repent of every sin I can think of, ask for a miracle.

'God, spare my son's life. Don't let the devil win,' I plead. On the way, I pass the mangled wreck of his motorbike.

Thank God he's alive and conscious. Only just, though. He's lost most of his blood and his leg is shattered. I dig deep for those hidden resources, suppress the turmoil and place a fatherly hand on his shoulder. 'Hello, Steve. It's me,' I say quietly.

A wan smile of acknowledgement from this former bundle of energy. 'I'm sorry, Dad,' he whispers.

A comforting stroke of his arm. 'It's all right, son. There's nothing to forgive. Don't worry. You'll be all right.'

We pray. The doctors come and I am ushered to the waiting room and a welcome cup of tea. I feel shattered, and the waiting has only just begun.

At last the doctor enters the room. I leap to my feet, a screwed-up ball of anxiety. 'His leg is very badly broken. The nerves are severed, the blood supply has gone. We will probably have to amputate the whole leg,' he tells me.

This is my moment of horror. Steve and I play sport together, we walk mountains. My mother had a leg amputated at the same age. Who knows what subconscious, ancestral memories flood from her spirit into mine? 'You've got to save his leg,' I beg. 'He's a sportsman, a young, active student with his life ahead of him. He couldn't cope.' The truth is, at that moment I can't cope. The surgeon makes no promises. 'We'll do what we can,' he says quietly.

Steve needed the motorbike to get to college. Like many young men of spirit in an age with few genuine rites of passage he needed the motorbike to express his coming of age. You know it's dangerous. Everything in you resists the idea. Yet, if we don't let our children grow up and take on the risks of adult life, there's the very real danger that they will later despise us, and with good reason. So, like many other parents, we lay awake every night until we heard the welcome burble of him arriving home safely.

Our son survived a five-hour operation performed by a skilled team of surgeons working through the night, but the future of his leg was touch and go. The church prayed. Those wonderful people devoted an entire service to him. One member said that he thought this was over-indulgent. He was wrong, and jealous. Those prayers, and the prayers of hundreds of friends around the world, accomplished miracles. God restored the missing blood supply and began a process of remarkable healing. All tribute to a surgeon who didn't take the cost-effective way out and amputate the leg, but heeded a father's plea and used his God-given skills to the full. But those prayers—so vital.

We quickly discovered that the immediate trauma was only the beginning. John was alone with Steve during the initial hours, but then together we spent weeks of twice, sometimes three times, daily visits to the hospital. There were further operations, skin grafts, bone grafts. The pain was appalling; the progress agonisingly slow. We later discovered that he had asked the doctors to amputate his foot. Thankfully, they refused. He was frightened deep in his spirit and had appalling nightmares. Maybe there was a satanic dimension to all this—a kickback because of the ministry he had been involved in.

He kept a brave, jocular face for the visitors. It hid the truth that he feared some Christians would not cope with—the truth that he was not rejoicing with indescribable joy, full of faith and the Holy Spirit, believing God for miracles and for the conversion of the entire ward. Instead, he was undergoing a painful bereavement process. His youthful hopes were dashed; his planned future was in tatters. He didn't even know if he would ever walk again. Where was God in all this? That was his reality.

He poured out his anger and frustration on us. It hurt like hell. We felt rejected. They were difficult days. Then came the truth that transformed the pain. 'I'm sorry. I can't help saying these things, even though I don't really want to. But you're the only ones I can really trust,' he said. 'I know I can say what I feel to you and you won't stop coming to visit me. I know you really love me.'

It was worth all the years of relationship building. We are his parents, the only ones he has, and he can be honest with us.

There were other honest times. Very late at night, when all the visitors had gone and the wards were quiet, Steve and John sat in the corridor and talked man to man. There were tears as he unburdened the pain of loss, the sadness and futility of what had happened. The healing would take time, but the process had begun.

Serious accidents come as a dreadful shock, but we accept that there is nothing premeditated about them. Time-bombs are different. We feel betrayed when they detonate. Our innocent assumptions are shattered. The bomb was planted long ago and somebody—God himself—knew about it and didn't tell us.

Every mother worries about whether the child she is carrying is deformed or not, and a sigh of relief greets the news that the newborn baby has a clean bill of health. We were no different from other parents when Sharon was born. Sure, there was a casual comment passed by the physician during one of the early routine check-ups: 'Your daughter has lordosis.' But we were assured there was nothing to worry about; that she would grow out of it. If only we had known.

To all intents and purposes Sharon lived a normal childhood. A bit accident-prone maybe, and with a tendency to break bones rather easily, but nothing too out of the ordinary.

It was only when she reached her teenage years that the time-bomb went off. A medical examination diagnosed that the lordosis was a corkscrewed lower spine with potentially serious problems. Bemused and stunned, we were introduced to the Boston Brace—a rigid polypropylene full corset with straps, designed to force the posture upright to prevent a worsening of the situation. It was agony for Sharon to wear this contraption day and night, and she bore the discomfort with amazing fortitude. But matters were to worsen. Incompetent physiotherapy damaged her back (not that we can prove it in law—can you ever?) and threw her into a spasm akin to the worst kind of slipped disc.

Sharon spent months lying in bed tanked up on painkillers. She lost the feeling in her legs because of pressure on the sciatic nerves. The back pain was unbearable and virtually untouched by the painkillers. These carried their own uncomfortable side-effects. Eventually she had a major spinal operation to remove some bone and cartilage.

Surgery is very good today, but operations on the spine carry the risk of further damage. We fretted, worried and prayed. She came through all right, but anxious days passed before we knew whether anything had gone wrong. Thankfully, things were no worse, but to our dismay nor were they really any better.

Her situation worsened over the months. School work suffered. Her social life deteriorated. The pain made her angry and depressed. She demanded attention, much to the chagrin of her older sister and younger brother. Eventually, she was virtually paralysed.

We spent days on seemingly interminable visits to clinics, hearing first this opinion, then that. A congenitally deformed vertebra was diagnosed as the cause of the trouble. Another major operation—a spinal fusion—might help. Clinging desperately to this one ray of hope to relieve our daughter's pain, we all but carried her to the surgeon. 'I can't do it,' he said, spreading his hands in despair. 'We can't afford to hire the nurses.' This was in London in one of the leading teaching hospitals in the country. 'If you could pay, I could hire the nurses and do it privately tomorrow. But it will cost several thousand pounds,' he added. It made us angry that we'd paid into the NHS all our working life—believing it would cover just such eventualities. We carried our weeping, pain-wracked daughter back to the car.

Eventually, speeded up remarkably by prayer, the surgeon was able to perform the operation. It brought wonderful release from pain and restored mobility—at least, for a good long while. Life became relatively normal, but it had taken its toll and we were to discover other problems associated with our daughter's back that were to prove equally devastating.

Yet, terrible as these problems have been, Steve wasn't killed by senseless terrorist violence. Nor even in the accident. His brain is not dead, and he kept his leg. He is now happily married to one of the nurses who sat with him beyond the call of duty and they have their first baby. He battled back into studies, passed an A-level, got a job, passed his car test, bought a house and is restored spiritually to much his former self. Although he has permanent damage to his leg and many scars to prove it, both legs are the same length and we have since walked mountains together.

For Sharon, too, it has not been all bad news. She is happily married to a wonderfully supportive husband, and together they handle the challenge with remarkable fortitude and good cheer. We have even seen one or two miracles in answer to our prayers.

We have shared these two experiences because many Christian parents and children undergo similar ordeals. Jesus taught that the rain falls on the just and the unjust. In other words, being Christians does not excuse us from the painful realities of life—it just transforms how we handle those realities.

Some people have a much harder time of it than ourselves. Teenagers do die. Some are paralysed for life. Many live with very serious deformities and disabilities. We have friends whose teenagers are mentally handicapped to the degree that normal communication is impossible, and there is no real hope of improvement. Exhaustion, guilt, anxiety and perplexity can drive us to the brink of despair. Where is the grace of God? How do we cope? How do we help our children cope? Teenagers ask real questions and we have to face these honestly. We and our faith lose all credibility if we don't.

Here are a few things we have learned. Be warned: they won't go down well with the 'Hallelujah, God wants you healed, and that's all there is to it' brigade. But they may help you and your kids who, like us, cannot duck the realities of faith and sickness.

The real question

We are among those who believe in divine healing. Many times we have laid hands on folk and seen God dramatically heal them. The church has witnessed miracles. In the family we pray about our normal complaints and God heals them. Our general health is better than most. And we can point to the scriptural basis for all this.

So what about our dilemma of apparently unanswered prayer?

Suffering, especially when our children are the victims, confronts us with raw, unsentimental questions: If there is a benevolent God behind the universe, how can he cause such suffering, or at least permit it to continue with such unabated fury against the young, weak, innocent and undeserving? If there is a God, is he not either impotent or the devil himself?

That may seem all too shocking a way for a Christian to frame the question. But when at times we cry in our anguish, 'Why, O Lord?' that is often the unspoken thought. Suffering confronts us with the choice of whether to abandon our faith and become cynical, grim-faced humanists trying to sort out the chaos of imperfect evolution, or of defiantly crying with Job, 'Though he slay me, yet will I hope in him' (Job 13:15). Our beliefs are on the line. Will we hope against hope? Will we believe in the reality of a loving heavenly Father, all-powerful, all-knowing and all-caring, even when the evidence seems to be to the contrary?

It demands a painful decision to look beyond the detail of our sufferings and to view the broader canvas of human existence. Yet when we do so, faith is released. In spite of our problems, we see that God is good. His glory fills the whole earth. We agree with the psalmist, 'I am still confident of this: I will see the goodness of the Lord in the land of the living' (Ps 27:13). The real battle is in making that decision to look up.

It is hard for our teenagers to do this when they are suffering, because they are not experienced at seeing life on the broad plane. Preaching at them, cajoling them, will not help. They need support and encouragement. When their faith wavers, we must cover them with our faith. There is nothing worse than an anxious parent trying to evoke the right spiritual signals from a suffering child. It is far better to be honest and say, 'I know you may not be able to pray for yourself at the moment, but I am praying for you. You've got enough to cope with without trying to be spiritual as well.' Give your poor child a break.

Whose sin?

It was said of the woman with the issue of blood that she had suffered much at the hands of the physicians. Unfortunately, many today have suffered much at the hands of well-meaning Christians. Job's comforters are still in business.

We've reacted. Traditional churches remember the sick at the prayer meeting and promise a better life beyond the grave. Now everyone is into healing. But, boy, are there some lessons to be learned. In few other areas have believers been so willing to abandon clear Scripture in pursuit of dubious pet theories that owe more to secular psychoanalysis than to the Word of God. Oh, the depths of soul-searching forced upon sick Christians who have come in all good faith to interminably long healing meetings, only for it to be implied in some subtle way that their illness is their own fault.

What do we mean? Here's some not-untypical testimony from our Sharon regarding her back problem:

> I found it very difficult when people prayed for me in healing meetings because they expected me to be better and I felt I ought to be, even when nothing was happening. People used to ask questions like: 'What's the spiritual blockage? Who haven't you forgiven? What's your big sin? Were you rejected as a child?' Or they'd talk about curses and want to cast out demons that weren't there.
>
> I found this very difficult because I thought they were getting at me and it undermined my spiritual growth rather than helped it. After all, I hadn't even had a chance to do any great sin, and I was born with the problem anyway. They made mountains out of molehills and never questioned whether it wasn't their own lack of power, or that the Holy Spirit just wasn't doing it this way.

It's very tempting to start analysing the patient for hidden causes when instant healing doesn't occur in meetings. This isn't what Jesus or the disciples taught. Sometimes illness does have its origins in sin, but more often than not it's just a fact of life and needs healing through the prayer of faith. If nothing happens, the sick person needs encouraging to have patient trust in God, not subjecting to more soul-searching for secret sins. He's probably had enough of that anyway.

If sin caused congenital deformities, then why do pagans produce perfectly healthy children? Surely theirs should be monstrosities! No, Christians who make these judgements do so either because they cannot accept the idea that God could allow suffering or because they are too impotent to heal it. Rather than face that, they project the blame onto those who can least defend themselves—the victims.

Don't ask why

It's very tempting in times of suffering to ask, 'Why is this happening?' But it's a very unhelpful question. Ever since Job's day people have been asking it, and the kindly answer from heaven has always been the same, 'You wouldn't understand even if I told you.' The question of suffering in general lends itself to some broad statements about the nature of the world in which we live, but the question of my specific, personal suffering can only be understood when seen from an eternal perspective. In other words, we have to wait until heaven—'then I shall know fully, even as I am fully known' (1 Cor 13:12).

Meanwhile there are far more constructive questions which can be asked and which will be answered now. Questions such as: What do you want us to do? How can we find your grace? How can we use this experience to help someone else? Real wisdom lies not in knowing all the ultimate answers, but in knowing how to live this day in the power of the Spirit and to the glory of Jesus.

There are greater things than miracles

It's tempting to want every prayer answered by a miracle. But think for a moment. After the initial thrill, we would very quickly take it for granted; simple prayer technique would soon replace our personal dependence on the Lord. Religion would become miracle-working ritual. We would cease to live by faith.

Hard as it sometimes seems, there is nothing more important than getting to know the Lord and trusting utterly in him. It is a learned process. And it's not for nothing that the sick are called patients. Perhaps it has become unpalatable today, but Paul writes, 'We also rejoice in our sufferings, because we know that suffering produces perseverance; perseverance, character; and character, hope' (Rom 5:3-4).

Although suffering is not essential for salvation in the sense that some treat it, nevertheless, it is one of the greatest stimuli to spiritual growth when we respond to it in a right manner.

We need a correct perspective on this. Someone recently said to us, 'You do have a lot of burdens to bear, don't you?' We don't believe that's the right way to look at it. Every trial that comes our way is another problem to overcome in the name of Jesus, not another weight to carry. It's what is under your feet, not what is on your shoulders that counts. That is the difference between the believer and the unbeliever. Stoicism or cynicism is the secular response; victorious faith is ours. If needs be, we'll mount our way to heaven on a pile of defeated problems. 'We do not lose heart. Though outwardly we are wasting away, yet inwardly we are being renewed day by day. For our light and momentary troubles are achieving for us an eternal glory that far outweighs them all' (2 Cor 4:16-17).

Real friends are real friends

The would-be healers we mentioned earlier were all well-intentioned. In no sense do we wish to criticise those who tried to the best of their ability. It's really a plea for discernment and for setting love above all our techniques and theories.

What we have found in our own church, and among many others who pray for us, is true love. Real friends are non-judgemental. They do not seek to be over-analytical and they never consider or make you think that you are a failure. What they do is pray, and bring words of encouragement, and occasional insights that may have some bearing on the problem. They are never condescending or locked into some unreal theology of healing.

Their love is practical. They send flowers, cards and chocolates. They cook a meal, do the washing and ironing, offer transport. Praise the Lord for such saints! We owed so much to so many people in our dark days.

Accept your child

Some parents apparently do not cope at all with this being the will of God. One of the most wicked men we ever came across was a man who claimed to be a Christian and was a member of a large charismatic church. We met him at a Bible week. His child had a serious deformity and the man bluntly refused to accept his child until God healed him. So the poor child received no cuddles, no comfort—only a massive rejection problem in addition to his physical difficulties. Such an attitude is worse than that of the pagans and an insult to the name of Christ.

Suffering children need all the acceptance they can get. Teenagers, who are beginning to think about life, the universe and all that, need it even more.

Children with deformities desperately want to please their parents. They try to be normal. Maybe they pick up the guilt felt by their parents and see it as rejection. Yes, we felt guilty—loving our daughter, yet sorry we had brought her into the world with such a problem. It's all too easy for teenagers, as they become aware of these things, to feel they are a burden on their parents.

Children with serious health problems often miss out socially. They can't do sport or travel easily. Teachers may not trust them. Yet they need trusting. The pain our Sharon endures is not constant. There are good days and bad days.

On the good days her naturally ebullient personality asserts itself to the full and there seems nothing wrong. The bad days have the opposite effect. If Sunday is a good day and Monday a bad day, do you trust her or do you imply that she is just trying to avoid school?

Children with problems also need the same respect as other human beings. Don't let your teenager keep the deformity as a dark family secret—it will make him feel a freak and he will be afraid of the news ever getting out. It is wrong to discuss a wheelchair-bound child as though he wasn't present. We have long felt that wheelchairs should have a lift mechanism to raise the victim to an eye-level contact with the rest of the world. What a difference that would make. Remember that children with mental illness can often understand far more than they can communicate back.

Pray without ceasing

Christian parents want their sick children to be prayed for. That is right and proper. We have seen many people miraculously healed through our own prayers and ministry. We have seen God do wonderful things for our children. However, do be prepared for the consequences. Ask your teenager if he or she wants to be prayed for. Don't just force them down to the front of the healing queue. Once you carried them; now, as teenagers, they must make their own decision. If they decide not to, don't criticise them for their lack of faith. A child may choose not to go forward because he is tired, or is feeling listless, or is coping with too many recent disappointments, or is embarrassed about his complaint being made public.

Recognise that not everybody is healed and that it's a mystery we have to live with. Don't allow any so-called healer to pronounce your child healed when the symptoms are still present and then claim the credit. That is a con. Don't accept the evil notion that it is the child's sin (or the sins of the parents) that has brought the complaint. Don't accept any suggestion that this is some punishment. Indeed you may have to refute this in your child's own psyche. Do thank the healer for trying. If he is an honest man he will feel as grieved as you if nothing happens, and you want to encourage him.

Finally, remember God's sovereignty. Job said, 'Though he slay me, yet will I hope in him' (Job 13:15). Yes, God does work miracles, but it is even more important that your child develops an unshakable faith in God's loving care and protection. That is what sustains all of us.

16
Hooked!

We may be oversimplifying the matter, but it seems that young people turn to drugs mainly for one of two reasons: either they are overindulged and bored, or they are emotionally deprived and lonely. They are seeking kicks or comfort. In both cases something is missing, and most commonly it is to do with the child's relationship with the parents.

If we have spoiled our children and taught them that life consists in having what you want when you want it, we should not be too surprised if they turn to drugs for pleasure. The bad example of an overindulgent lifestyle on our part, coupled with giving them too much cash and freedom, is inviting trouble.

On the other hand, if we neglect our children's emotional well-being, if we nag and abuse them, if we are too busy to spend time with them, then we run the risk of their turning to drugs in an attempt to fill the gap. Rejection is fertile soil for comfort-seeking experimentation. This can be a particular and painful problem for children growing up in a single-parent family.

Children can be driven to experiment with drugs either to enhance their academic or sporting performance, or because they cannot cope with the expectations placed upon them and they need a way of opting out. It is one thing to wish our children to do well in education; it is quite another to send out subtle signals which suggest that their warm-hearted acceptance by us is performance- related.

Because we might be the cause of the problem, we may be unaware of what is happening. Many otherwise decent parents are shocked when they find that their son or daughter is experimenting with drugs. 'How could it happen to our child?' is the common cry. Nevertheless, it can, and we had best be aware of the dangers.

Before we examine ways of protecting our children from the all-too-obvious dangers of drug addiction, it will help to explain what we mean by the term.

Substance abuse

The existence of drugs is not the primary problem. It is their abuse that leads to corruption and self-destructive lifestyles.

All potentially addictive substances have their origin as part of God's good creation. For example, the bonding power of certain molecules produces the adhesive holding this book together. Glue-sniffing is an abuse of the substance. Nicotine is an excellent environmentally-friendly insect-killer. Heroin, as diamorphine, is used to control pain in terminally-ill patients. The printing process produces the Bible, with its exaltation of sexual joy within marriage. The same process is abused when it is used to produce pornography. Chewing the leaves of the coca plant enables Andean Indians to live at high altitudes. Men abuse it when they turn it into crack for sale on the streets.

Although we need the authorities to control the availability of certain addictive substances, censorship is not sufficient. The would-be addict will only find something else to abuse.

Not all abuse leads to addiction. This is because not all drugs are addictive, nor do most teenage users reach the stage of dependence. Even if they do, we have to distinguish between psychological dependence and physical dependence—the former is the most likely.

In spite of the publicity, relatively few addicts die. Those who do are more likely to do so because of an accidental overdose, or because they mixed drugs (alcohol and barbiturates are a lethal combination), or because they had a drug-related driving accident.

Defining dependency drugs

We can only mention here some of the potentially addictive substances presently available in our society. The advent of designer drugs (laboratory-created compounds designed to enhance moods) means that new pills are constantly coming onto the market, and who knows what new commonplace substance people might suddenly discover gives them a high?

Tobacco—the slow killer

The single most destructive drug habit in society is tobacco-smoking. Nicotine and the accompanying volatile chemicals are lethal, and the practice causes more illness and death than almost anything else. Nearly 30% of people are now addicted to this legal poison which is promoted as a healthy, socially-fulfilling habit. Nicotine is a stimulant drug that paradoxically can also relieve anxiety and stress. Used over a period of time, tobacco slowly poisons the body until is becomes highly susceptible to cancer, heart attacks and other degenerative diseases. Tobacco is one of the most addictive of all drugs and each cigarette smoked is estimated to reduce life expectancy by five-and-a-half minutes.

Alcohol—the challenge of moderation

If the wine that Jesus and the disciples drunk was not alcoholic, why did Paul command Christians not to get drunk on it? Without entering further into the debate, the consumption of moderate amounts of alcohol is permitted in the Bible as one of God's blessings, and current medical opinion is that modest consumption alleviates the risk of heart attack. However, like all blessings it can be abused and we live in a society where over-consumption causes death on the roads, violence in homes, bust-ups at soccer matches, and a disturbingly high number of unplanned sexual encounters at parties. Alcohol is a depressant drug with the potential to destroy health and reason if used to excess over a long time.

Pornography—sex without love

Pornography is addictive. It is also socially isolating, as most porn is watched in solitude and accompanied by masturbation. It can be very time-consuming and the masturbation may become compulsive. Pornography alters our perceptions about love and people, reducing love to copulation, and men and women to amoral animals. The insistent message produces sexual obsession that may lead to prostitution, promiscuity, rape and adultery. People addicted to pornography often have difficulty in forming healthy sexual relationships within marriage.

Video games

Recent years have seen a spate of ever more sophisticated leisure games for computers, and some companies are making a fortune out of it. These games can be great fun and some teach logical skills and help improve reaction times in the participants. Arguably, arcade games, by occupying bored teenagers, help keep them out of trouble.

However, some kids become addicted to these games, often simply because they try endlessly to beat their previous high scores. Certain games of the 'Dungeons and Dragons' variety worry Christian parents because of the occult associations of the fantasy worlds and the increasingly interactive role play required of the participants. Although some susceptible children may be at risk of psychological or spiritual damage, the greatest danger is simply in the enormous consumption of time involved in this non-physical and often solo activity.

Food—gluttony or anorexia

Many parents worry about their teenager's eating habits. To one child it's, 'What? Are you stuffing your face again? You're overeating. Look at you. You're getting fat!' To another it's, 'You must eat. Are you worrying? You're not becoming anorexic, are you?' Poor kids who have to live with such fretful parents.

Thankfully, and contrary to what the popular media implies, there is no such thing as the standard human body or metabolism. Some people will tend to leanness, others to obesity. Teenage children have ravenous appetites at times. They also go through periods when they are indifferent to food. Occasionally, they try silly diets. In most cases natural hunger redresses the balance. However, there's no doubt that some children become comfort-eaters. This often manifests itself as an addiction to sugary and starchy foods. A few children become addicted to *not* eating. Food becomes repugnant and may even induce vomiting. This may indicate anorexia, which needs urgent medical attention before the patient starves to death.

Obesity is a slow crippler and killer. Seriously overweight teenagers often have problems of self-rejection. Many find it difficult to be fashionable or to engage in sports.

Fun drugs—designed for passing pleasure

Party poppers are chemicals that raise the metabolic rate and enhance or, in some cases, alter consciousness. They are passed for sale at parties, and include amphetamines, LSD, 'magic mushrooms', Ecstasy and other designer drugs. Few are truly life-threatening or addictive in themselves. The dangers come from accidents arising from bad trips or physical over-stimulus to the heart. All such drugs have a depressant after-effect. It is this that may create a psychological dependency.

Barbiturates—bedside suicide?

Common painkillers are found in most homes, whether as aspirin, ibuprofen or paracetamol. Many girls take them for period pains. They are one of the most common ways of taking an overdose in the 'cry for help' suicide syndrome. For minor pain relief, encourage the use of aspirin or ibuprofen rather than paracetamol, because large doses of the latter can destroy the liver irreparably, even if the patient survives a suicide attempt. Barbiturates and sleeping tablets are used to reduce stress, and in some cases are taken in a suicide attempt. Physical dependence is a reality with these drugs, and sudden withdrawal can be fatal.

Cannabis—mellow marijuana

Cannabis-smoking induces a state of relaxed euphoria. This enjoyable human condition normally occurs when our circumstances turn out wonderfully good—usually as the reward for hard work. Cannabis produces the feeling without the work, and psychological dependency develops, often resulting in a drop-out lifestyle because one of the prime motivators to work (the pleasurable reward) has been short-circuited by the drug. However, cannabis is not addictive and the long-term effects are more likely to be similar to those associated with tobacco-smoking.

Cocaine—gets up your nose

Cocaine is an expensive white powder extracted from the coca shrub. It is either sniffed, or is smoked as crack. It is a powerfully stimulant drug producing exhilaration and indifference to pain or fatigue. Sometimes it induces anxiety. The after-effect is one of fatigue and depression. Psychological dependence can develop.

Glue-sniffing—smashed on solvents

Certain commonly-used glue solvents and aerosol propellants, when inhaled, produce a similar effect to short-lived alcoholic drunkenness. Gases squirted directly into the mouth can cause suffocation and heart failure. Users are likely to experience a hangover and generally lose their ability to concentrate.

Steroids—performance at a price

Anabolic steroids increase muscle size and male aggression. They are a temptation to those heavily committed to performance sports and are easily obtained in many private gymnasiums. The drugs can restrict normal development in the young and in women. They reduce sex drive.

Heroin—needled to death

Heroin is the best-known killer drug, but addiction usually comes about through the use of other, less destructive, drugs. The principle is important to understand. Once a dependency pattern is established, whereby good feelings can be obtained by using an outside artificial stimulus, your child is vulnerable to harder drugs.

Heroin produces severe physical and psychological dependence leading to social breakdown. The craving for a fix drives many victims to theft, prostitution and violence. Association with fellow-addicts results in health degeneration, including AIDS transmitted by sharing infected needles. Impure supplies, accidental overdose, infection and poisoning can lead to death.

The signs of addiction

Albatrosses are rare; seagulls are more common. In other words, the fact that any of the symptoms we list below might be present at any given time in your child's life does not mean that he or she is necessarily taking drugs. Most kids do not. There is far more likely to be a less dramatic, 'it's only a seagull' explanation for their behaviour. It is important not to panic.

However, if there is a marked and prolonged change in behaviour pattern that includes several of the following factors, then you should investigate further.

Mood changes

This may be from cheerful alertness to sullen moodiness interspersed with unexpected irritability or aggression. This might be accompanied by extreme restlessness and sleeplessness, or by persistent drowsiness. Your child may become disinterested in life, indifferent to food, hobbies, sport, school or work. Personal habits may be neglected.

Change of friends

Your child may become involved with other drug users and begin to spend long periods of time hanging out with them.

Old, 'square' friends may be dropped. Your child may be secretive and evasive about these new friends.

Tell-tale signs

Money or belongings may disappear. You might become aware of unusual smells on your child's clothes or body, or in the bedroom. Small plastic bags, pieces of tinfoil, unusual tablets and powders may be found. Your child may appear to have the symptoms of a continuous cold.

There may be a simple explanation for the above. It might be just a moody phase, or 'calf love'. It might be more serious. If it is, then you must talk with your child and seek help as soon as possible.

A community problem

Most children who become involved with drugs do so because of an inner need that is not otherwise being met. This is the root problem that has to be tackled. However, the fact that they turn to drugs as the way of trying to resolve their inner need is a community problem. Somebody has to supply the substance. This might be a shopkeeper selling alcohol or tobacco to under-age children, or another adult providing the goods. You may yourself have failed to set a good example in this area.

Sniffing usually takes place in the company of others. Pushers sell drugs at parties. The customs police have limited success in preventing the import of hard drugs.

This means that when we seek to help our child we have to look at all the outer sources as well. How is the child getting the substances? What company is he keeping? Where does the money come from?

It will probably be helpful to talk to the year head and

form tutor at school. They may already have noticed a decline in school achievement. Help from a local community drugs project may be usefully sought. The police may not be the best initial recourse because they are obliged simply to uphold the law, which might mean you and/or your child being charged with possession, or with allowing your premises to be used for drugs. Fear of the law and its consequences is unlikely to be an effective way of handling your child's inner problems.

Immunisation is better than isolation

The pressure to experiment with addictive or potentially addictive substances is a real one. Kids are offered soft drugs at parties, in the playground and at friends' houses. Many young teens consider tobacco-smoking to be macho. Tall stories about getting smashed on vodka at a party encourage indulgence in alcohol. Pornographic books, videos and magazines circulate freely among both boys and girls.

A typical parental reaction may be to attempt to protect our children by isolating them from all possible sources of contamination. Up to a point there is wisdom in this. Certainly there are insalubrious events which are best avoided. We should be selective about the videos we allow them to watch, particularly those which are violent and sexually exploitative.

However, this may simply produce a reaction. Ultimately we cannot protect our children by isolating them. Some parents attempt this by public school education only to find that the problems are as rife there as in an inner-city ghetto school.

Immunisation is the only sure way to resist disease. That means we must create an immunity within our children.

By education

They need to know the dangers. Wise parents teach their children from the book of Proverbs.

> Do not set foot on the path of the wicked or walk in the way of evil men. Avoid it, do not travel on it; turn from it and go on your way. For they cannot sleep till they do evil; they are robbed of slumber until they make someone fall. They eat the bread of wickedness and drink the wine of violence (Prov 4:14–17).

Children should be encouraged to choose their company with care. Paul writes, 'Do not be misled: "Bad company corrupts good character"' (1 Cor 15:33). There are times when it makes sense to walk away from the gang.

It is good to advise our children of the health risks associated with drug-taking—though we must recognise that this will have less appeal to them than to us. Remember too that although all drugs are bad, they are not all equally bad. We must get our facts right.

Any drug habit, whether addictive or not, is going to prove expensive. If we have taught our children how to handle money properly, and if we set sensible limits on their pocket-money, they will probably get the message.

By secure relationship

We cannot stress enough how important it is to ensure that our acceptance of our children is not based upon their performance. Some kids turn to drugs simply because they are worried about their exams and about pleasing their parents. Healthy encouragement and motivation is one thing; making them perform to receive our good favour is quite another matter.

Some children make friends more easily than others. Members of a healthy, outgoing group are far less likely to develop drug problems than loners, or those who join a socially alienated group. Church youth organisations have a major role to play in this.

Children from single-parent families are often emotionally vulnerable. They, perhaps more than many others, need the benefits of a good structured youth club where they can find acceptance and encouragement in a pastorally secure situation.

By purposeful living

If church is a boring, non-challenging spiritual sedative, then our kids will be tempted to experiment with more exciting alternatives. The faith should be at its most demanding for teenagers. We should tap into their idealism and energies. Encourage your children to care for others, to involve themselves in evangelistic outreach, to seek to know God for themselves. Teenagers with a real sense of purpose to their lives have no need for drugs.

17
Trouble at School

By the time your children reach their teenage years, you may well have become used to an unenthusiastic response to your question about how school went today. Most children find little to get excited about over algebra, physics, general studies and history. Much more interesting is a riot, an arson attempt or a teacher having a nervous breakdown in public. Fortunately for teachers, these things don't happen every day.

You will also get used to the fact that many teenagers appear to give scant regard to their homework. You may wonder if they are learning anything at all. Before you panic, remember that many teachers set less homework now than they used to when we were young. In any case, most of us did as little as necessary even then, didn't we? And can we really expect children who leave home at 8.30 am and don't arrive back home until 4.30 pm then to start the evening shift? Most of us find that difficult enough as work-hardened adults.

These are the common concerns about school and a quiet word with the form tutor will usually set our minds at rest.

School shyness

There can be more serious problems. If you detect that your child is becoming morose about school, or is developing regular excuses based upon tiredness or ill health, then it is worth investigating further. It might be pure idleness—although don't forget that teenagers need more sleep than adults because so much of their energy is being consumed in growing up.

It may be that your child is becoming school shy. If so, you need to discover the reason.

Bullying

Unfortunately, bullying is commonplace, and some kids endure years of misery because of it. A few have tragically committed suicide.

If you detect that your child is a victim of bullying, your first recourse shouldn't be to rush to the school to complain, as this will most likely have negative results. Try to find out why your child is on the receiving end. Quite possibly he just needs to stick up for himself.

Children from Christian homes are usually taught pacifism by example because Christian parents don't resort to violence. This can be especially difficult for boys, and your son might get a reputation for being a wimp. Although we do not advocate getting into brawls, none the less a show of toughness is often enough to deal with the matter. Our Steve helped one victimised boy by doing weight training with him. The extra muscle not only provided some deterrent to the bullies, but it gave the boy the needed physical self-confidence. After all, bullies only go for those whose spirits they perceive to be weak and vulnerable.

Do make sure that your child isn't bringing it upon

himself by taunting, teasing or being a general pain in the backside to his class mates. You'd be amazed.

Racial harassment is a different matter. It is illegal for a start, and very harmful because it strikes at the root of our ethnic identity. We cannot change the colour of our skins. Most race prejudice is perceived as whites against blacks, but white children can be just as harassed in black/Asian environments as the other way round. However, do check that it is truly racial harassment before plunging into the fray. The fact that your skin is a different colour doesn't mean that every bit of bullying is for that reason. If you are certain that it is a case of racial harassment, then you have the right to seek legal redress.

If, for whatever reason, the bullying is serious and beyond your child's ability to cope, then you should intervene strongly. Begin with the form tutor, but if it doesn't stop be prepared to approach in order the year head, the head, the school governors, the local education authority and the police.

Teachers themselves can be the bullies on occasions. They are more likely to do so verbally, though physical abuse is not unknown. A sarcastic teacher is a bad teacher and should probably not be in the profession. Authority based upon earned respect, a sense of humour and genuine care for the pupils is the only kind that truly succeeds. Some teachers, unfortunately, do take things out on particular children, and some have their obvious class favourites.

Again, before charging in with accusations, do check the facts carefully and thoroughly. Children have selective memories and often, even though they may be honest, they are seeing things only from their own limited perspective. Usually, talking the matter out in the presence of the teacher is sufficient. However, if you are unsatisfied with the outcome, you should press for disciplinary action against that teacher.

Bad company

You may find that your child is being accused of causing trouble, because he is part of a gang. The desire for acceptance and excitement is strong in teenagers—and school can be incredibly dull. When we were at school, members of our years set fire to the buildings, broke windows, let down car tyres, set off stink bombs on buses, beat up other school gangs, stole their property, went on sexual escapades, indulged in shoplifting, played truant and generally made a nuisance of themselves. Nothing changes, except that you don't want your child to be part of it. The message of the book of Proverbs is plain: 'My son, if sinners entice you, do not give in to them . . . my son, do not go along with them, do not set foot on their paths' (Prov 1:10,15).

Don't accept hearsay evidence. If serious accusations are being made against a group of teenagers that your son or daughter normally associates with, demand proof that they were party to the alleged offence. It is all too easy (though understandable) for irate plaintiffs to blame everybody in sight. Just because a child wears the same uniform doesn't mean he is guilty.

You may, nevertheless, have to face the fact that your child has been skipping school and has got into trouble. What are you going to do? The Bible speaks about the goodness and severity of God. It's a helpful clue to our approach. You will want to stand by your child and do all you can to help. But you will want to lay down the law about his future behaviour in no uncertain terms. The authorities will be much more likely to treat the case leniently if you take this approach and they can see that you are responsible parents. Nevertheless, you may find that expulsion from school, a heavy fine, or even a custodial sentence is prescribed nowadays.

It is better to avoid the rocks in the first place than to risk shipwreck.

Performance fatigue

School shyness also occurs because children are finding it difficult to keep up with the work. This may be because the course is too difficult. The GCSE programme tries to ensure that children find their own level, but like all such systems it is imperfect. The real crisis is more likely to come at A-level. In our opinion, A-levels are more difficult than university degrees. Usually a child has to take three subjects, will need good grades, and has only two years to accomplish all this. University degrees are more focused and allow three years. Not surprisingly, numerous children crack up under A-levels.

If there are problems at any stage in your child's school career, then it may be worth discussing whether he is doing the right course of study. How easy it is to want our kids to follow in our footsteps, or to do the subjects we wanted to do but couldn't. It is important that they make their own choices. Guidance we may give, but not dictation.

Sometimes there is a conflict between the curriculum possibilities and what a child is really good at. A change of school may be the only real answer, but that must be carefully weighed against your child's social development.

There is a tendency among the predominantly middle-class section of the church to think that all Christian children should be academics. However, this is not true to the facts. It also fails to recognise the nobility of manual work. Many a child will do far better obtaining a job and working through to a comfortable position, than by struggling on at school. Indeed, some professions favour this approach. Don't let your child become a performance-driven workaholic in his teenage years.

Unemployment

We live in a time when there are not enough jobs to go round. The reasons for this sad state of affairs are complex and include government inertia, widespread recession, technological advance, geographic redistribution of labour and the lack of war.

It can be a hard time if your child cannot find employment. Rightly or wrongly, many people still assess their usefulness in life by whether they can hold down a good job or not. The money helps, too.

Unemployed teenagers can become very depressed with fruitless visits to the job centre, scouring newspapers, making phone calls and writing letters to which they receive no reply. You will have them moping around the house all day and showing all the signs of restlessness. The next stage is apathy—and that is even worse. What can you do?

Positive action

A good CV has become a necessity these days. Encourage your child to produce a positive statement about himself. If you don't know how to do this, seek advice from others within the Christian community who do. Find someone who can type it up properly, and make a number of photocopies.

Encourage your teenager to keep his or her options broad. The first job is the hardest one to obtain. It need not be the only job they will ever have. A year or two of work experience in almost any job will be a major asset in seeking the work they really want to do. Some of the most successful people in our society did a variety of jobs before finding their settled career.

Remind your child that failing to get an interview is not a personal rejection. There simply aren't enough jobs to go round and short-lists are drawn up by employers having to handle far too many applications. Those who persevere are eventually likely to find something.

Keep looking in the newspapers. Write to the major employers in your region. Many will keep a reasonable application on their books for several months, even if they have nothing to offer at present.

Pray for the right door to open. Encourage your child that God cares about these practical things as well as what goes on in church.

Unpaid employment

The devil finds work for idle hands—so does God. The fact that your teenager may not have a paid job does not mean he has to be unemployed. There are many voluntary agencies crying out for help, and much of this can be wonderfully rewarding. It stops your child from vegetating and will enhance his self-worth. The church may also have a number of activities where the unemployed can serve usefully.

Further study

Whether to go for more qualifications or not is a vexed question. The extra years of study do not guarantee a job at the end. However, the right course can make all the difference—not only to the academic type, but also to those who are best suited to learning a trade. Some job-related skill under the belt, a touch of initiative, ideally some capital, and your teenager might just start up a business of his own.

Unemployment is a major problem in our society, but before we become too discouraged, it's worth remembering that most people who want a job, and who persevere, get one.

Even more homework

Discuss with your teenager the problems of suffering.
 Talk about drugs.
 Ask your child what he or she thinks makes a good friend.

Part Five

Faith, Fellowship and the Future

18

Passing on the Flame

It's sometimes said that there is no such thing as a teenager in the Bible, and if we mean by that the jeans-clad, Madonna-mad, exam-swotting, globe-trotting, disco-bopping creatures that we have produced, then we agree. You won't find *them* in the Bible.

At the same time, the Scriptures do recognise the time of life that we call the teenage years. So when we encounter the word 'youth' in the Bible, we can equally read it as 'teenager'. Thus, for example, we can paraphrase Psalm 119:9: 'How can a teenager keep his way pure? By living according to your word.'

Or Psalm 144:12 might be rendered: 'Then our sons in their teenage years will be like well-nurtured plants, and our teenage daughters will be like pillars carved to adorn a palace.'

The psalmist's prayer touches one of the deepest desires of any Christian parent's heart. It is that our children should come into our faith and grow to love the Lord and serve his church, for the whole of their days. The one thing that threatens to break our hearts more than anything else is that our children should, upon reaching adulthood, reject the faith of their fathers and go the way of the world.

It's not automatic that our children should enter into a personal adult relationship with God. The fact that we produced them does not guarantee their salvation. Any theology that says otherwise is unreal to experience and fails to take account of what the Scriptures teach. On top of that, it is downright dangerous—we can hardly afford to be complacent about their eternal destinies.

Our children need to hear the gospel and to respond to the claims of Jesus Christ upon their own lives. It is vital that they experience genuine conversion. They may not have lived lives of great social evil, but they are still sinners in need of salvation. No one attains heaven by virtue of a decent upbringing—not even the Pharisees could manage it.

Childhood professions of faith can be very real and lasting. It was the case with all three of our children. But the gospel doesn't end with conversion. Jesus calls us to be his disciples. That means learning to be like him and to do his will in our adult lives. As our children progress through their teens, they will be confronted repeatedly with the challenge of what this means for them.

The demands of Christ must not be watered down. There isn't a special, modified gospel for teenagers, any more than you find a special gospel for women, or for men, or for one-legged monkeys. Jesus calls every one of us to radical discipleship, total life commitment to him. And let us not forget that the disciples who first heard him were largely young men and women.

It's tempting to play upon the idealism and emotional susceptibilities of young people and to produce an evangelical easy believe-ism. A happy-go-lucky, gutless Christianity can give leaders some flattering instant results, but it'll all be over by the time the 'converts' reach their twenties. True Christianity is a life-changing call to sacrifice, devotion and heroic deeds. Let's not con our kids into accepting a plastic replica which will melt as soon as the heat is on.

Parental responsibility

The prime responsibility for all this lies with us parents. Excellent as many youth leaders, youth camps and conferences are, we mustn't leave the job to them.

Deuteronomy 6:4-9 says:

> Hear, O Israel: The Lord our God, the Lord is one. Love the Lord your God with all your heart and with all your soul and with all your strength. These commandments that I give you today are to be upon your hearts. Impress them on your children. Talk about them when you sit at home and when you walk along the road, when you lie down and when you get up. Tie them as symbols on your hands and bind them on your foreheads. Write them on the door-frames of your houses and on your gates.

Every Christian agrees that we should love the Lord our God with all our being. But we must also impress these things upon our children—not in religious gatherings, but in the context of everyday life. This is the true religion of the wayside. The things of God should arise naturally in our conversation as we chat at our meal tables, as we walk or drive, when we're on holiday or traipsing round the supermarket.

Proverbs 22:6 says: 'Train a child in the way he should go, and when he is old he will not turn from it.' It's a double-edged verse. If you train a child faithfully in the ways of God, then when he is old he will not turn from it. But, if you train a child badly in the ways of God, then when he is old he will not turn from that either.

If you say, 'Well, we think kids should make their own

decisions. We're not going to force religion down their throats. They can find out for themselves when they're old enough, if they want to,' then you are training a child in the way he should go—and when he is old he will not turn from it.

Parents with this attitude are training their children to believe that the Christian faith isn't really that important. Cleaning your teeth is important, so is eating your greens and going to school. But worshipping God is something you can take or leave.

If you've been a believer for some time, you will hopefully know better than this and will have taught your children the gospel of the grace of God. They will have learned to pray on your knee. You will have guided them in how to read the Scriptures and given them an understanding of its major truths. By now, they may know how to worship in the Spirit, how to serve the Lord and how to witness. Probably at some point your child has made a profession of faith.

All of that is good, but it isn't enough. We keep coming across adults who, having had a Christian upbringing, for one reason or another fell away during their teenage years.

In the last century there was written, and often sung, a hymn that seems excruciatingly sentimental to us today. It was called 'Where is my wandering boy tonight?' But the hymn reflected the anguish of many a parent whose child had rebelled against the faith. We may not sing the hymn any more, but there are still many prodigal sons, and anxious parents continue to grieve over their spiritually-wayward children.

Of course, you may be a very recent believer yourself. Your children may have come into the faith with you. One of the greatest difficulties you perhaps face is the unfamiliarity of being spiritual together. It can seem strange and embarrassing to start talking about the Lord when your life to date has excluded him. This is especially so for English people because for some strange reason religion remains an embarrassing topic of conversation.

However, overcome this natural shyness and you have all the freshness of new-found faith to experience together. Both you and your children can enjoy the exciting adventure of discovering all about the Lord. Although you do not have the advantages of long Christian experience, you may nevertheless gain some wonderful insights as to what it means to be a Christian family. In fact, you may progress faster than some who have grown complacent because of their many years in the church.

However, if your child is an older teenager and still not a believer, you will have to be more cautious. It's no use imposing a religious veneer on the life of a household if your seventeen-year-old son doesn't want it. He will only react with anger and make life miserable for everyone.

He feels something strange and alien has happened to you. What he needs to know is that you are still the same parents who love him and share the common ground you have always shared. That's the best way to reach him for the Lord. No pressure, no imposition. Just love, friendship and normality. Whether he comes to the Lord or not may well depend, not on your ability to preach to him, but upon your success at becoming a better friend to him.

It is often heard from certain platforms today that our children will do greater exploits than we. In one sense that may be true. For example, our own children, like many others, were not only saved at an earlier age than we were, but they were baptised in the Spirit, speaking in tongues, prophesying, witnessing, having visions, seeing miracles, long before ever we were into those things.

We praise God for all the good things experienced by

recent generations of children. But it will take more than this if they are to bring about a significant change in the spiritual climate of our nation. The road of Christian discipleship is long and not without its pitfalls. Triumphal songs may help the march, but our children, like us, still have to walk with their feet, not their mouths.

We can help them. There are certain common factors at work in teenage Christian lives. If we understand what these are and know how to feed into them at appropriate points, our children have every chance of coming through with flying colours.

Training and testing

In his first letter, the apostle John draws a parallel between natural growth and spiritual growth. Children in the faith, he says, know that God is their Father. They also know that their sins are forgiven. Fathers in the faith know 'him who is from the beginning', that is, they have a mature personal relationship with Christ, the Eternal One.

God's will is that we should progress from childhood to maturity. To do so, we have to pass through adolescence.

Whether or not we attain to maturity in the faith depends on what we make of this phase in our spiritual development, so the apostle explains what characterises a good spiritual teenager: 'I write to you, young men, because you are strong, and the word of God lives in you, and you have overcome the evil one' (1 Jn 2:14).

The illustration applies, whatever our natural age might be. It's to do with how much we have actually grown in the faith, not just the number of years we have been alive as Christians. We've met folk who have been forty years in the faith and never yet grown out of their nappies. Others, though converted only a short while, grow by leaps and bounds.

The reasons for this vary. Some remain immature because the level of teaching in their churches never gets beyond the breast-milk stage—comforting, nutritious in its way, but not suited to spiritual adulthood. Others refuse the discipline of spiritual adolescence and so never develop the capacity for a mature relationship with Christ.

Although, as we say, spiritual growth isn't simply to do with the number of years we've been around, none the less, there is a certain parallel. For example, if your children gave their lives to the Lord at quite a young age, then it's entirely possible that the challenge of spiritual adolescence will hit them at the same time as they enter their natural teens.

Teenage years are spiritually a time of exercise, a season of battle training, and a period during which their minds are being renewed by the word of God. It's a time, if you like, when they are winning their spurs. This is when they must qualify to become true disciples of Jesus.

If all goes well, they will come through no longer fickle or naïve in their faith, but with the steadfastness of those who have been properly coached for spiritual warfare.

Every teenage Christian has to engage the enemy during this time. The conflict is usually on one specific topic. It will appear to be a major issue for the one enduring it.

Sometimes the testing is in the sexual realm—a fight with lustful masturbation, pornography or heavy petting. It can be over a boyfriend or a girlfriend. Or it may come as a lure to covet something—an obsessive craving for a motorbike or an expensive stereo, for example. Your child may even be tempted to steal.

The battle may be in the realm of personal identity— pride or, on the other hand, self-pity and inadequacy. As we've seen earlier, some children wrestling with these issues are tempted into taking drugs—cigarettes, alcohol abuse, glue-sniffing, cocaine, 'pot' or heroin. Suspect this and you need to act fast if a tragedy is to be averted.

Whatever the trial, the outcome is crucial to our children's spiritual future. Yet, for all our care and concern, we may hardly be aware that the battle is taking place.

Jesus went into the wilderness for his fight with the enemy. Nobody saw, nobody helped or comforted. It was his battle. The devil tested him on three key issues: the lust of the flesh, the lust of the eyes and the pride of life. There could be no 'destroying the works of the evil one' in the lives of others until the Son of God had proved that those works could not take control of his own life.

He overcame by the word of God, and sent the devil scuttling. It wasn't the end of the war, but the battle was a crucial one. Jesus returned from it in the power of the Spirit, ready now to wreak havoc on Satan's kingdom and to usher in a new era of salvation.

So it must be with our children. They have to learn in their own experience that they can win. It's a bit like taking on the playground bully. Sooner or later, this young thug gets to duff up everyone in the class. Your Johnny is wondering when his turn is going to come. Then one day the bully shoves into him. 'Oi! Who're you pushing? Looking for a fight, are you? Right, I'm going to punch your face in!'

There's no one else to hand. Your little kid has to handle this alone. If he runs, he is only putting off the evil day. If he quails, the bully will win and continue to terrorise him for life. What is he to do?

He may be frightened stiff on the inside, but outwardly he sets his jaw. 'All right, then. If that's what you want.'

And before the bully can make a further move, *wham*, your kid gives him a right-hook in the midriff. Down goes the thug. (It will help if your child has prepared somewhat for this eventuality!)

That bully will respect your child in the future; he knows he packs a punch. More important, little Johnny no longer lives in fear and trepidation; he knows that this bully isn't as tough as he makes out.

In spiritual terms, children have to discover the power of the word of God, the sword of the Spirit, against the subtle reasonings and violent threatenings of the devil.

When John writes, 'And the word of God lives in you,' he means that the word which is written on the page of a Bible has become prophetic; it has become the living word of the Spirit in our own hearts. God's word is now ours also.

Let's illustrate it this way. A man used to shoplift before he was saved. He did not stop shoplifting simply because the Bible says, 'Thou shalt not steal.' New Covenant faith isn't a matter of looking up the rules and thinking, 'I mustn't do that any more,' and then engaging in a lifelong fight against our own desires. The new birth instils something much more potent in us: God says, 'I will write my laws on their hearts.'

When a regenerate man reads the truth, the Holy Spirit witnesses it to his renewed spirit. The man agrees in his heart that shoplifting is wrong. He himself no longer wants to do it. He has come to agree with God. God's word has become his word. It's not mere outward conformity but inner conviction.

During their teens our children will learn what this means for themselves. Truth we have taught them will begin to make sense in their experience. The choice as to which voice they obey will bring into focus the true desires of their hearts.

As with all times of training, there are good days and bad days. Remember when you were trying to pass exams? One day you sit down and it actually seems interesting. You study and things make sense. Some of it even goes in. Another day you stare at the book and think, 'I've been reading that line for an hour now, and I still don't know what it says, let alone what it means.'

The same is true when you're training for a sport. There are days when everything goes right, and those when everything goes wrong. One day you wish this was the championship because you're performing so well. The next, you feel you'd be better off taking up crochet instead.

It's just the same spiritually. Our children will have their ups and their downs. Sometimes they will make enormous strides in a very short time. At others, they will seem hardly to have started at all. That's typical of any training time in life.

Part of learning is, of course, finding out for oneself. The insecure person is frightened to experiment for fear of getting it wrong. But those who make no mistakes seldom make anything at all. Experimenting and taking risks are what progress is all about.

When we bought our computer, we went through the manual very, very carefully step by step, frightened that we were going to wipe the program out at any minute. When our Steve uses the computer, he doesn't even bother with the manual. In half an hour he's mastered most of it anyway. Bang, bang, bang on the keyboard. 'Try this, Dad. No, try that. It doesn't matter if you lose it 'cos you've got a backup. What we need is to change the parameters on your EMM386.EXE so the device includes the segment-base address D000h. Put that in your CONFIG.SYS, and try to get your syntax right this time! No, you don't need shadow ram. You're better off with a cache.' If this sounds like gibberish. . . .

Steve learned by experiment. He was less fearful of getting it wrong than we were. So he knows more—about computers anyway!

In the spiritual realm this can give us anxious parents some worries. For example, your child may suddenly decide not to go to church one Sunday. He wants to go out with some mates instead. Holy panic! Is this the end of his faith? Or is it just an experiment? You may even find out that he sacrificed going to church to try and win his friends to the Lord. A right fool you'll feel if you start an earnest exhortation about 'not forsaking the gathering together of yourselves' the moment he walks in the door, only to find out that his friends are coming with him to church the following Sunday.

She might want to go to another church. A church not like yours, heaven forbid! What's going on? Just another experiment. As likely as not your daughter will return full of enthusiasm. 'Isn't our church wonderful? I never knew it was so good until I tried that other place. It was so boring! I'm not going there again.'

Of course, she might have found it much better. In which case, you have something to learn about the reasons why.

However painful it is for us when they appear not to be reading their Bibles, not praying, not wanting to go to church, not enjoying the worship, sitting in the back row chewing gum, we have to let it happen. They must find out for themselves what they want. Certainly, it's inappropriate by the time a child reaches fifteen or sixteen years of age still to be dictating their leisure time on these matters.

What they are asking themselves is, 'Do I really need this faith? Do I really want this lifestyle?' Quite likely the devil is asking them those questions too—and offering some juicy alternatives. Pray for them.

Where are the role models?

We've already mentioned that we think teenagers need a good sexual role model in Mum and Dad. But they are looking for role models in all aspects of life. Hence the success of the cults. One of the major reasons why teenagers become enmeshed in cults such as the Moonies is because there exists a charismatic personality at the top.

What kind of role model are you? Teenage years, more than any other time, will test and expose hypocrisy in the home. As we've indicated throughout this book, they are watching our behaviour like hawks. They are challenging to see whether our faith is good enough; whether it's true, or whether it's false.

And they will tell us off. It's an uncomfortable experience, and one that we will be tempted to resent. When children are young, if they tell you off or accuse you of anything, you rebuke them. 'Don't be rude! Don't you dare speak like that to your mum. If you do it again you'll get a good hiding!' But when they become teenagers you have to listen—not to flagrant and unwarranted rudeness, but to what they're picking up. 'You're always so rotten miserable at teatime, Dad. All you do is moan. It's the same every day.'

Tempted as you are to retort, 'Don't you speak to me like that! How dare you say I'm miserable?' you must hold your tongue, because they are probably right. Six o'clock in the evening is a bad time for many of us. Worn out from work, being depressed by the news, trying to eat your meal, and they want to ask questions about whether they can go with some friends to Finland in October. They want to know whether you will pay for it, and whether you will arrange for someone to drive them to the airport at three o'clock in the morning because it's a cheap flight and won't cost you so much money if you do that.

It's no easy matter to move from demanding a proper respect from your children to having to repent because they've actually spotted something inconsistent in your Christian life. It's much easier to go back to the old defensive role model of parent and young child than to say, 'Sorry. I guess you're right.'

Teenagers observe, and they say what they feel. Much of the time they will be devastatingly right. It's uncomfortable, but you have to take it. Take note: if you are carnal, then why should they be spiritual? If you cannibalise the preacher over Sunday lunch, then why should they ever respond to biblical teaching? If you criticise people in the church who are not doing things right in your eyes, is it surprising that your kids grow cynical about those same people, and develop fault-finding attitudes?

They are looking for consistency and reality in their parents, so it's no use going all religious and plastering every wall and shelf with texts. Nor is it any help to adopt a pious super-spirituality. 'Hallelujah, the milk's boiled over!' 'Praise the Lord, Johnny's just fallen down the stairs and broken his leg!' Choruses all day long will drive your kids barmy. 'Hallelujah anyway!' or the more refined, 'The Lord knows,' when the tank bursts, the door falls off its hinges, you trip over the cat and bring the washing down on your head, will turn them off. Especially if on other matters you are less 'spiritual'.

What is really needed is a consistent demonstration of spiritual integrity and honesty in the home. That means being open about our faults as well as our good points.

Children are impressed, not by our chorus-singing, our

platitudes and texts, but by our humility and our willingness to say, 'I've got that wrong. I'm sorry.' They are blessed when we make the long journey up to their room where they are sitting, reading a book with some head-banging music pounding through their brains, lift off the earphones and say, 'Sorry I was ratty down there. I didn't mean to be, but I was. Please forgive me!'

Our ability to be honest over our failures is more important, we believe, than any other single factor. Kids really can't cope with hypocrisy and double standards in their parents. Honesty truly is the best policy at home—and everywhere else.

This isn't to say that our children always get it right, or that we should for ever be telling them how bad we are. As we've stressed before, part of the problem of youth is simply the lack of experience and perspective on life. But they get more right than our parental pride likes to admit, and we will do well to try and learn from their observations, even if they are a little over the top at times. In fact, your teenagers can be a greater means of bringing conviction to you about where you need to improve than all the sermons your pastor preaches in a year.

All this is more important than our texts and choruses—and even family Bible studies. As families grow up it becomes quite difficult, if not impossible, to maintain a 'family altar'. In the past, you may have liked to gather for a reading and prayer at the breakfast table. Now, everyone gets up and leaves the house at different times. If your child doesn't have to go in to school that day, he may not get up at all.

One of the practical things we tried to do every so often (it has to be said with limited success), was to break bread together as a family. Sometimes it can be done by making

Sunday lunch the one good family meal when you're together.

If family prayers are no longer practicable, then praying for one another at all sorts of other times is vital. We pray for each other whenever there's something that needs praying about. We don't wait for a family time or a special moment in the day. On the stairs, in our rooms, by the kitchen sink, we pray for and with one another. The Lord is real and he's not confined to meetings over the meal table or meetings in church.

The best role models our children can have is of parents who are honest, genuine believers who quite naturally bring the Lord into all aspects of their daily life, without recourse to any form of religious artificiality. Children of such parents will always feel they can talk about their own spiritual experiences without embarrassment or fear. They will learn how to be naturally supernatural.

Others will have their part to play, of course. Youth leaders, pastors, respected Christians will all have something to contribute. And it's good for our children to be exposed to the influence of truly godly people. But there's no substitute for our role as parents.

19
Spiritual Awareness

Oh, the joy of young glands and open minds! Excitable, energetic teenagers awash with hormones at the merest stimulus of the Spirit, ready to go to the ends of the earth, to change the world, to topple the giants and usher in the kingdom of God. Not for nothing did Peter proclaim, 'Your sons and daughters will prophesy, your young men will see visions' (Acts 2:17). No spiritual sexism here! 'Upon your teenagers, girls and boys, will I pour my Spirit,' says the Lord.

While old men dream, youngsters are getting hyped-up with visions of a glorious future. Their zeal may well make us feel our age.

You have only to watch them in their meetings. Young Christians praise God very, very energetically these days. They're jumping up and down shouting, 'Praise the Lord, yeah, yeah, glory to God!' You're bracing your legs for one feeble hop, gasping, 'Puff, pant, yeah, puff, glory!' as best you can.

We were in a meeting some time ago where, at the appeal, hundreds of young people surged forward. It was not a young people's meeting as such and when a member of the platform party asked, 'Hey, what about the old ones?' there were hundreds of older folk who put their hands up because they knew they too should have come forward. The teenagers demonstrated more zeal for God, more honesty, less self-consciousness about whether they would be 'looked at' than did the older people. That is typical of teenage years. It's possible to obtain incredible responses from them because they are so open and enthusiastic.

However, they're still immature. And, as we've stressed already, it's no sin to be so. The difficulty for us parents is that there will often appear to be a contradiction between the vision our child is getting at church and the fact that he won't tidy his room.

'Cor, Mum, we had a fantastic time at youth group tonight. It was incredible! We laid hands upon everybody; we all felt hot and cold and shivery inside and Bill freaked out on the floor for half an hour. We stood around him holding our hands over him. He was laughing and chuckling and he was flinging his arms, and then Sheila—she screamed like mad and started dancing round the room. It was fantastic!'

'Done your homework?'

'Aw, Mum! I haven't had time. You know that. And I don't have to do it until next Thursday.'

'I thought you said it had to be in tomorrow?'

'Wellllll. Well, he's a lousy teacher anyway.'

'But you need to study for exams and a job.'

'Aw, come on, Mum. You never get a job when you leave school anyway. What's the point of bothering with it? Besides, I'm going to be a missionary after tonight, and I don't need to work for that. You're always going on at us about our homework. I'm fed up with it and I'm going to bed. So there!'

What happened to the glorious time at youth group?

How we handle this all-too-familiar scene is ever so crucial. It's tempting to down on them and to wipe out that spiritual experience as being totally over the top and unrealistic. Sheer hypocrisy and all that.

But do we really want to knock their admittedly immature expressions of faith? Should we not be grateful that they're showing their enthusiasm for God rather than for the local football club or some vain pop star?

Earlier in the book we said we would explain why Christian young people find the lure of Romanticism and rock so hard to resist. The reason is simple. Rock culture offers emotional satisfaction. It's images, the driving beat, the chance to dance, the hype and glamour—it's exciting. A rock concert is a corporate 'spiritual' experience, a celebration of life and energy, an occasion of cosmic worship. Compare that to your average church service.

Unless our children can be allowed to experience emotionally the reality of God in their lives, we'll lose them to the prevailing alternative—or they'll grow up deadly dull. Whatever we might make of modern trends in Christian worship, there's no doubt that freer styles have greatly helped our young people feel they have something going for them that's every bit as good as the rock culture. In fact, most of them will say it's far better.

However, it still won't guarantee tidy rooms or completed homework. This ability to have incredible feelings and experiences yet somehow not to connect these with the reality of homework and room tidying, is simply a matter of immaturity. It's actually only a teenage version of what is true in so many of our lives.

We can go to church and praise the Lord with all our hearts. But what happens when we get back for lunch? The meat is underdone—or incinerated. Husband stomps up the garden muttering something about starvation. Wife resents the fact that he didn't even lay the table. 'Cutlery will be rusty by the time we get to eat at this rate,' he mutters. She reaches for the tin of baked beans. 'Serves you right!' she fumes.

What's so different? Except that we should know better, and should probably apply the word 'sin' to our reactions.

It's the same as going to work on Monday morning and finding the whole office or factory is in chaos and people haven't done what they should have done. You're feeling fed up, cheesed off with the whole thing and it shows. That's only the adult version of immaturity. We all have to learn how to connect our spiritual experience with the reality of our daily lives. The last thing you want from your husband or boss is, 'Call yourself a Christian, you rotten hypocrite!'

Our kids can do without it as well. Here is a better approach: 'Darling, it's terrific that you had such a good time at youth group tonight. I'm glad you enjoyed it so much. Let's pray that God will enable you to take that into school tomorrow and demonstrate it in your work and in your relationships.'

'Oh, er, all right, Mum. Yeah! Well, I was just going to go to bed now. I'm feeling quite tired.'

'Well, we'll just pray about that. Let's ask God that the things the Spirit is doing will enable you to do your homework. Let's pray that somehow the Holy Spirit will have an effect upon your room. After all, you don't want the angels tripping over everything, do you?'

You'll probably get a wry smile to acknowledge that they've taken the hint.

Speaking of rooms, how many parents have arguments with their kids about the state of their bedrooms? Probably more cross words are exchanged over this than almost any other subject. Many of those words are needless.

It may help to know that there are, broadly speaking, two types of mind in this world. We'll call them the mind of the accountant and the mind of the artist. Those with the former tend to think in tidy compartments, in neatly stored boxes, in order. They make excellent researchers, being superb at fine detail, accuracy and the like. You want a surgeon who thinks like that. Such people probably have tidier rooms than most of us.

Those with the artist's mind think associatively. Their heads are full of ideas and memories all thrown in together. But just say the right word and it will connect with the thing you want. These are the creative thinkers, the people of ideas and insight. They make good prophets. They are seldom tidy.

Most of us are a mixture of both types of mind and, without overstating it, are usually mid-range when it comes to tidiness.

Here's the point. What is more important: that things are laid out neatly and in order, or that we can find what we want when we need to? And that's the test of whether your child's room is truly chaos or is just an associative but workable jumble. Can they come up with the goods? Does the homework turn up? Or is it always lost first thing Monday morning? Can they come out dressed reasonably clean? Are you sure there are no mice and no strange coloured things growing down the walls, or under the bed?

We're not suggesting you give your children licence to live in chaos, and certainly not in filth, but we do recommend you allow them to express their own mind in the way they live. All of us appreciate a bit of space that we can call our own and in which we can be ourselves.

We suggest that you might make a reasonable house rule that at least an hour a week is spent on cleaning and tidying the room, including returning other people's things that they've borrowed. That will keep the mess down and the morale up. And when you conduct room inspection, try not to say, 'What a tip! Have you done anything in the last hour?' Unless it's true, of course. And the way to check that out is to inspect before and after.

This time of spiritual awareness mustn't be despised. God will work many things into their lives during these years and although we may wince at times, we should not be too judgemental. Better your children get high on Jesus than on drugs, sex or violence.

And there will be a genuineness about their faith that can be quite startling.

One day our daughter, Sharon, and her fiancé arrived home at our nearest railway station, three miles away, only to find they had no money to phone for a cab, let alone to pay the taxi fare. So they prayed.

The woman in front of them at the phone booth said there was 15p credit left if they wanted it. That took care of the phone call. The taxi duly arrived and, just as they were getting in, penniless, a stranger approached, enquired as to their destination, found it was on his route, asked if he could share their cab, and said he would pay the fare in full! Not bad, eh?

Questions, questions, questions

Some churches seem to be nothing but questions. Questions about doctrine, questions about the way the pastor runs the show, questions about unanswerable speculations, questions about what the young people's group get up to. The one thing not permitted is a clear, authoritative answer.

Other churches, particularly those which have embraced a certain form of authority/submission teaching, may not permit questions at all. Doctrine is as delivered, the church is run as the elders dictate, all initiatives come from the top. Even though such churches do not as a rule impose their authority in a cultish manner, none the less, creative investigation is at a low premium among the membership.

Ideally, a church should recognise both the place of spiritual authority and the place of exploratory learning. People should not be in rebellion, but neither should they be discouraged from asking intelligent questions.

We need to engender such attitudes in our teenagers. Certainly, we must beware of panicking or becoming overly defensive when they want to ask serious questions about the faith.

Teenagers' spiritual questions tend to fall into three broad categories: those about what the Bible actually means, those concerning the big social issues of the day, and those to do with the life of the church.

The first sort are fairly easy to deal with. If you don't know the answer yourself, refer them to a good Bible dictionary or commentary. Failing that, recommend they speak to the pastor. After all, he's meant to be the expert.

The second kind are more difficult. For example, here is a common question they might ask: 'If there's a God of love, if he really loves, then why does he allow all this suffering in the world?' Or the other version of the same problem: 'If God is all-powerful, more powerful than the devil, why doesn't he stop the evil that's going on?'

Fair questions. And it is proper that they should be asked. Our children are trying to relate their faith at its interface with everyday world experience. They're not simply rebelling, and we must not treat them as though they were. Instead, we must seek to answer them with the simplicity of wisdom.

For example, when there's a major transportation disaster, like a ferry sinking, you could respond by saying, 'Isn't the devil evil to do that? But isn't God good that it happened on a sand-bank and not more lives were lost? And he inspired so many courageous people who managed to get there and do such wonderful work in saving people's lives. Isn't man arrogant that he gets so careless about his own abilities that he doesn't put sufficient safety checks in to his operations?'

That's relating faith and experience. It's not answering the whole question of why God allowed the thing in the first place—we don't pretend to have an easy answer to that one—but it is a way of broadening out the initial question so that our children can see there is more to it than meets the eye. It won't do simply to blame God.

Take the famines in Africa as another example. You might approach it like this: 'Aren't we arrogant in this country? We have more than enough food. In fact, there is enough food to feed every mouth in the world, but we are so greedy and selfish as a society that we let these people starve. We could easily afford to ship out millions of tons of grain to them, but we won't do it. Instead, we're cutting back on our farming, we're reducing our output because we're too efficient and producing too much. Rather than give it to the poor, we're reducing the amount that we produce. Isn't that evil?'

Help your children see where the real problem is. The West has failed to recognise that its ability to produce an excess of food is a stewardship from God to enable the starving to be fed as well. That's sin.

And the answer to sin lies not in violent political revolution, but in the transforming power of the gospel. Not only do individuals need it, but so does society as a whole. We must challenge this wretched institutional evil with the love and mercy of God. Get out there and start sharing it, kids!

Answers of this kind provide our children with a bit more ammunition for the debates they encounter at school and college, and they are reassured themselves that their faith is relevant to the modern world.

The range of social questions is vast and undoubtedly confronts the church with its major challenge for the next decade. John's book, *Issues Facing Society* (Harvestime), tackles the major ones. Let's not be afraid to give our children militant answers. After all, this is spiritual warfare.

The third kind of question revolves around church life. Why are things run the way they are? What's wrong with Mrs Jones? Why doesn't our church allow this, that or the other? These are the most sensitive questions, for they draw us in at the level of our own prejudices and opinions. Wise restraint is called for, as well as honesty. It's all too easy to allow our own feelings to colour the answer we give, especially if we ourselves are dissatisfied with the way things are going. A bit of intelligent criticism on our part may be interpreted by our children as permission to dynamite the pulpit.

For all that, don't discourage their questions and observations. They can often see things with clearer eyes than we can. One of our children once devastated us with an observation about the worship in our previous church. He said, 'Dad, where's the Holy Spirit gone in our church? Our worship is just a chorus sandwich.'

We were taken aback. We had not used such a phrase in our child's living memory. In fact, we had last used it in about 1972 when we had abandoned hymn-sandwich type services in favour of a freer and more biblical pattern. Our son, however, had perceived that things had slipped into another rut.

It drove us to prayer. Steve wasn't rebelling; he was perceiving. We needed to seek the Lord over it and pray, 'Lord, let your Spirit move again. Let us not settle for a new liturgy. Let us not come into another kind of routine that neglects the Holy Spirit.'

Let the questions come. Both parents and children can learn from them. And if we feel ill-qualified to give the right answer, let us ask God for wisdom. Unlike intellectual expertise which depends upon intelligence, wisdom is given to all who ask—and often the less intelligent, not relying on their own understanding, receive a whole lot more than the brainy ones. A comforting thought for all of us.

20

The Will of God

Do your children know the purpose of God for their generation? Are you able to tell them what it is, or even to enable them to discover it for themselves?

Although there may be some differences of opinion over what has constituted the will of God for our own generation, some things are reasonably clear. (We take it that God is not helplessly looking on while we mess around with our own petty ideas. He is the Lord of history, and of his church in particular.) For example, there has been a considerable rediscovery of worship in the Spirit in the past twenty years. Although the forms have varied from church to church, there is no major grouping of churches left untouched.

A renewed emphasis upon the work of the Spirit in the life of the believer and the re-emergence of spiritual gifts should also be noted. It has led a significant number of churches to adopt new and arguably more biblical structures of life together, not least including the release of the laity to minister in areas such as home groups. And a fresh challenge to re-evangelise the nation is coming rapidly to the fore. There is much else besides.

If you have been an active Christian for any time, you will have been a part of all this to some degree or other. But, good as it may have been for us, it does not constitute the will of God for our children. We must beware of simply putting them through an action replay of our own history. That would be to turn their Christian lives into a game of charades.

In the progressive church tradition from which we come personally, our children do not have to discover how to replace legalistic quiet times with Spirit-filled devotions. It's not necessary for them to find out how to substitute vibrant worship for the hymn sandwich. They don't need to be taught about house groups and Ephesians 4:11 ministry patterns. All these matters were the concern of our earlier years.

Time rolls on. The issues change, the lines of battle move. This up-and-coming generation needs to hear God for itself. Proverbs 29:18 says, in the Authorised Version, 'Where there is no vision, the people perish.' And it's true. If we wonder why teenagers sometimes seem bored with church, it's because they have no vision. Nobody has effectively communicated with them what their part is in the purposes of God.

When we were young believers, once we knew our spiritual role we were gripped. Nothing else mattered. All our energies went into fulfilling this glorious challenge. So it must be for our children. They need to know the hand of the Lord upon them for their own generation. Otherwise, the present widespread awakening will fail and yet another spiritual revolution will be needed to mobilise the church for the hour.

The problem is even more acute for those in traditional churches. Thousands of young people grow up in Sunday schools, attend youth organisations and church services, but never make it into adult church membership. Why? Because nothing gripped them.

We do not have the space to enlarge upon what we think

God's purpose is for this new generation of Christians; nor is it altogether appropriate that we should, because teenagers must feel themselves to be part of the process of discovery. They don't simply want to be told what their elders think they should do.

However, it most certainly requires them to get very much more involved in society than we have. They will have to take on the powerful institutions in our land. In the process, they will probably experience levels of persecution different from that which we have undergone. A resurgence of mission is called for, but of a totally new style, both in this land and throughout the world.

We can encourage our children to explore these matters with one another. Teach them that the Christian life isn't just a hobby. Most important of all, assure them that they have a role to play in the future of the church, and it starts now.

This broad perspective perhaps concerns church leaders more than parents, though we have our part to play. However, what about the specific will of God for our children's individual lives? What about studies and careers?

Success and sacrifice

Do we expect our children to succeed? What do we mean by success? How is it measured? Many Christian parents come from rather middle-class backgrounds or have evolved into middle-class lifestyles as a result of conversion.

It's trendy to knock this, and usually the people doing so are themselves middle class. Not having the courage to forsake their comfortable lifestyle themselves, perhaps they shout righteously about the virtues of working-class Christianity to appease their consciences.

Consider for a moment, however. You may have been a

debtor, with no idea of how to manage money, no wisdom to speak of, and then you became a Christian. You committed your financial state to God and he gave you wisdom. You began to give to his work and he started honouring you. Before you knew it, you were out of debt and saving. Gradually, your lifestyle began to improve. You've become comfortably well off. Because you appreciate that it's by the grace of God, you probably handle this with a good spirit.

There's nothing wrong with it. In fact, it's a testimony. However, the problem may come with your children. They have inherited your comfortable standard of living, quite likely with no real appreciation that it came about as a direct result of living by faith. The danger is that they will simply adopt secular middle-class values and expectations as the way things are.

Do we give them to expect that success means automatically buying a house, rather than renting or, horror of horrors, living on a council estate? Is it understood that they are going to get nine GCSEs and three A-levels, go to university or college, have a good middle-class job? Is that what we mean by success? Or are we open to the possibility that the will of God might be rather different?

We are not adopting some pseudo-left-wing position by saying this. Nor are we anti-success. We believe God calls people to be very successful and to go to the top. Indeed, we pray that Christians reach positions of real power and influence in our society. And every good parent, quite rightly, hopes their children will do well in life.

However, we must be careful that we don't just lay our values unthinkingly on our children. Supposing the Lord calls them to lay down their lives for the gospel? John brought a prophetic word at a young people's conference concerning forsaking everything we have to follow Jesus. He did his best to make the appeal as difficult as possible to respond to. He tried to get folk to sit down, even after they had stood. He emphasised the cost.

For all his efforts, a large number of young people responded very seriously to the call. But the real cost for many was to do with their Christian parents.

John had young people coming to him in tears the next day saying, 'I wanted to stand, but I couldn't pay the price of how my Christian mum and dad would respond to the idea of me giving up everything for God. They have career expectations for me and would be appalled at the idea of me being a single missionary, possibly even losing my life for Jesus. I'm not afraid to do those things for him, but I know how my parents will feel.'

It demonstrated the spiritual depth of some of those young people that they feared they might have missed the boat by not standing up the previous night. One guy said, 'I would want to stand up now 'cos I've prayed this through over night. I've agonised with God and I'm prepared even to take on the antagonism of my parents. Can I be counted in among those who stood to lay down their lives for the Lord?' Yes, he could. And difficult as his parents might find it, they had actually done a fine job in producing such character in their son.

We mention this, not to frighten every parent who reads these pages, but because we recognise the seriousness of the call of God upon some young people's lives. A number may even die for the Lord. Some of them will give up that career and those qualifications. It will mean sacrificing marriage for some—and that means no grandchildren, Mum.

This is not necessarily going to be the will of God for everybody by a long chalk. His purpose for most of our children is that they get married, live in the same sort of houses as we do, and have kids just like we did. That is as much a part of the kingdom of God as full-time ministry. All we're calling for is a willingness on our part to release our children into whatever God has for them—and that may not be 'success' as the world counts it.

We must remind ourselves that, years ago, we dedicated our children to the Lord. We said, 'Lord, thank you for the gift of this child. We return the gift to you, and we receive from you a stewardship to raise him for you.' Whatever the words or ceremony, that's what we meant. Our children's possible futures may now test the truth of our promises.

Career choices

Once our own hearts are clear on this, we are able to guide, help and advise our teenagers. We must talk through study options, career possibilities and work opportunities. Of course, let's take advantage of the Careers Office and any other advice to hand, but we need to be involved, too. After all, we know our children very well. And, most importantly, we can bring in the vital spiritual dimension concerning the will of God.

We need to discuss matters with our children's teachers as well. Parents' evenings are useful, but don't be afraid to call in at other times. A good teacher appreciates your interest; a bad one needs it. Mind you, your child may well complain like mad about you interfering and do his best to put you off going.

'It's no use seeing Mr Cobblebrain. He's thick! He doesn't even know who I am. Anyway, whatever he says, it's because he's mixed me up with someone else. And you won't understand what he's talking about anyway. Come to think of it, he left last term, and the new teacher's deaf and dumb, so I don't even know his name.'

Take not a blind bit of notice. Mr Cobblebrain will probably turn out to be charming, passably intelligent and even quite helpful.

The number of choices today is quite bewildering, and the pressure to specialise early on is a very real one. For this reason, we shouldn't be worried if our children can't make up their minds what they're going to do in life. Indeed, the chopping and changing of ideas is quite a healthy process. Far better that than to be like the girl who has made up her mind from childhood that she's going to be a nurse, only to find that she isn't accepted at the interview, and is then left completely without a clue as to her future.

In spite of the apparent pressure to have everything sewn up, it's perfectly possible for teenagers to change courses, take a short-lived job or two, and still get it right in the end. We must be careful not to stream our children too narrowly, too early. Our own daughter, Debbie, took two jobs doing little more than data entry before joining the Health Service and qualifying as an audiologist—a job she found thoroughly satisfying. If anyone had asked her when she left school if that was what she planned to do, she would probably have had to ask them what an audiologist was.

One of the acid tests of any study course or career choice must be, 'Do you really enjoy the work?' That's not to say it won't be hard at times, but is it generally enjoyable? There's little point in a child struggling with a subject he never really liked in the first place.

We have found the following questions useful to ask our children when we've had periodic talks about their futures. You may think of others.

1. What do you like doing?
2. What are you good at doing?

3. Do you prefer to work alone or in a team?
4. Do you want to produce a product or work with people?
5. What sort of working environment do you favour?
6. Do you want a manual or a desk job?
7. What do you think God is saying?

Such questions help bring clarity. It is then a matter of exploring the possibilities together. And as you do so, encourage your children to pray continually, 'Your will be done.'

Actually finding a job is a story in itself, as we've indicated earlier. The possibility frankly depends a lot on which part of the country you live in. Unemployment is a real threat to many and the constant struggle to find work can totally destroy a teenager's self-confidence.

Children need our support and prayers at such times. They also need our encouragement not to mope around all day, but to find useful things to do. Churches in depressed areas really ought to construct voluntary work programmes and even small businesses for their unemployed young people.

Many children have no problem at all and quite enjoy the challenge of applications and interviews. Most still appreciate a few tips on how to go about it. Today, presentation and self-confidence are quite as important as qualifications. That is where we parents come in.

Before full-time work commences you may have to face the vexed issue of their getting a part-time job while still at school. We touched on this earlier in the book. The money, of course, will be welcomed by all—you especially as it means you can stop shelling out a small fortune in pocket-money. But it does need to be weighed against other things, such as how your child is doing at school, how tired he gets, the impact a job is going to make on his social life, and so forth.

You may have to resist the pressure for a while until the right sort of job comes up. And even when and if you give in, keep an eye on it. Many bosses exploit juveniles in ways that are actually illegal and can cause them to suffer real stress.

Discouragement

You may be reading this and saying to yourself, 'It must be great to have children who are spiritually aware, asking questions, finding out the will of God for their lives. But my kids aren't like that at all. They're bored silly with the whole business. What am I to do?'

Just about all kids go through phases of unresponsiveness. Usually, it's because they have grown discouraged with life. There are several reasons why this might be.

Overdemand

It's surprising how many teenagers there are, from Christian and non-Christian homes, who feel they've fallen short of expectations.

Christian young people may feel they should be more spiritual. Although their parents have never vocalised it, they pick up a sense that they've let the side down. If studies have been linked with spirituality, then they may feel a disappointment in their schoolwork as well. Often this feeling of failure is particularly with regard to their fathers.

It is so important that we reassure our children that they're all right. For example, when ours have been taking exams, we have always made it clear to them that if they succeed we'll say, 'Praise the Lord!' And if they fail, we'll still say, 'Praise the Lord!'

We never gave them grounds to imagine that their acceptance depended upon their passing exams. Yet, even then, such is the pressure today that they did on occasions feel it was so. We all have to work hard at constantly reassuring our children of our unconditional love for them.

The same goes for spiritual or physical performance. Worship and service must spring from the heart, not from a desire to gain acceptance with parents. Sporting or musical accomplishment is very fine, but we must beware of using their standing with us as a lever to make them perform better. 'We'll be so proud of you if you win,' carries with it the unspoken consequence, 'We'll be so disappointed in you if you lose.' It's wrong to put this sort of pressure on our children.

Let your kids know that you accept them because you love them—and that's good enough. Keep telling them that, because they live in an age and at a time of life when people are making great demands and are often putting them down if they don't succeed.

We've been appalled, for example, by teachers who have made children feel worthless because they didn't come up to their expectation of them. That is so evil. Teachers who use cynicism and sarcasm as weapons are poor teachers and unworthy of the trust placed in them. It does terrible harm to young lives. As we said earlier, don't be afraid to complain.

Overbusyness

Teenagers can become discouraged just because they've become too busy. They're suffering from burn-out. It's amazing how much energy they can consume, not only with activity, but also because their bodies are still growing. An endless round of meetings, social activities, sports and parties, coupled with a run of late nights, can be quite sufficient to produce a drop in spirits.

This is the time when you need to insist on some early nights and some nights in. Never mind the complaints. They won't like it, but you'll probably find within a few weeks they're feeling much better and the spiritual sparkle is returning. Sometimes a few vitamins and some iron tablets for girls can help, too.

Secret sins

It's not unusual for youth leaders to have boys confessing to masturbation problems and feeling they've blown it spiritually. The subject, as we've indicated in the section on sex, needs to be openly and sensitively talked about.

It may be, of course, that the sins of others have stumbled them, notably people in the church. They may have picked up on unjust criticism or thoughtless speech. Because teenagers don't always get it right, some older folk are apt to convey to them that they've always got it entirely wrong. That can be very discouraging to youngsters. You have to deal with these matters, not simply by taking sides, but by helping them to forgive—and by assisting them in seeing where they unwittingly offend others.

Where is God?

They might feel let down by God. We have to help our children understand what the Lord is doing with them when he appears not to answer their prayers. It can be confusing, to say the least.

We've written earlier about the tough time our Sharon has with back trouble. On occasions, she has felt quite mystified about the will of God. She's gone forward at healing meetings where the speakers have claimed that God is moving by his Spirit and doing all sorts of wonderful things. People have laid hands on her. She's fallen down and shaken, rocked and rolled or whatever else people do in these meetings, and still she's not healed.

Discouragement isn't very far off at such times and it requires of us wise counsel and support. Coping with apparently unanswered prayer is a problem for us all, and learning how to handle it is part of growing up in the Lord.

On the whole, teenagers are robust creatures. They do get discouraged, but they have remarkable powers of recovery. Provided we are sensitive to their needs and are there at the right time, these phases soon pass. Only if depression becomes a way of life do we need to probe deeper and call in some outside help.

Just occasionally, discouragement can lead to open backsliding. It's a terrible pain for parents to watch powerlessly as their child rebels against the faith and becomes just like his non-Christian school friends. A child in that state can become quite intolerable, perhaps blatantly smoking, swearing, blasting out the heavy rock; in fact, demonstrating thoroughly that he has rejected the Lord.

What matters most in such unfortunate circumstances is that you continue to love your child. You will never win him back to God by withdrawing your affection. Love, self-restraint and prayer are the way. Like the father of the prodigal son, you must wait in faith. One day, you'll see in the distance a dust-covered figure drawing towards you. . . .

The last word

The trouble with the last word is that it can't be written. There is always something more—especially when it comes to teenagers.

In Malachi 2:15, speaking of the marriage covenant, the prophet says, 'Has not the Lord made them one? In flesh and spirit they are his. And why one? Because he was seeking godly offspring.'

The most important thing that we will ever do is to pass on the flame of godliness to the next generation. Our most vital work is to produce future saints and servants of God.

We hope you've realised that this cannot be achieved in isolation from everything else. The relationship that we spoke about in the first section is crucial. We also have to help them handle the reality of living in this world. We need to tackle this very big area of sexuality and sexual behaviour. Life will not always be easy or turn out as we expected. We must stand with them in the process of discovering the will of God for their lives.

We didn't set out to answer all the questions or to provide an exhaustive manual on teen-rearing when we started this book. It can't be done. Rather, we've tried to suggest an approach, an outlook, and some guidelines to follow—along with a few pitfalls to avoid. We've sought to be sympathetic and encouraging. For all that, you may feel inadequate, not to say a bit of a failure.

Virtually every parent does at some point or other. And that should encourage us. There's no such creature as the perfect parent. What we have are a lot of people doing their best, not losing heart, managing these years, day by day as they come. Along the way there are times of success and times of failure. What we've modestly tried to do is provide the means of avoiding disaster with a bit of divine wisdom.

That, in the event, will prove sufficient. Follow the Lord's ways and your children will love you, even if at times they show it in strange ways. One day, they will bless you for your firmness and your understanding—most of all because you were there, and you cared.

So be encouraged, weary, wondering pilgrim! God's grace is sufficient for this task. Pour your nerve tonic down the sink and pray. You'll be pleasantly surprised at the outcome. Indeed, it could turn out to be really good fun most of the time.

Psalm 145:3-4 declares: 'Great is the Lord and most worthy of praise; his greatness no-one can fathom. One generation will commend your works to another; they will tell of your mighty acts.'

God will help us to pass on this heritage to our children. Opposition abounds, but the Lord's power is perfected in weak but willing parents such as ourselves. Can we do it? In his strength we can. God bless you as you do so!

Postscript
You could do worse than let your teenager read this book. At least he or she might get to see your side of the picture!